BIG ENGLISH 3

Mario Herrera • **Christopher Sol Cruz**

Contents

BIG ENGLISH
♫ Song ♫

From the mountaintops to the bottom of the sea,
From a big blue whale to a baby bumblebee—
If you're big, if you're small, you can have it all,
And you can be anything you want to be!

It's bigger than you. It's bigger than me.
There's so much to do, and there's so much to see!
The world is big and beautiful, and so are we!
Think big! Dream big! Big English!

So in every land, from the desert to the sea,
We can all join hands and be one big family.
If we love, if we care, we can go anywhere!
The world belongs to everyone; it's ours to share.

It's bigger than you. It's bigger than me.
There's so much to do, and there's so much to see!
The world is big and beautiful, and so are we!
Think big! Dream big! Big English!

It's bigger than you. It's bigger than me.
There's so much to do, and there's so much to see!
The world is big and beautiful and waiting for me . . .
    a one, two, three . . .
Think big! Dream big! Big English!

unit 1
Every DAY

1 **Listen and read. Then sing.**

Kate Can't Be Late

It's Monday, 7:30.
Kate is still in bed.
Her mother sees the clock and says,
"Wake up, sleepy head!"

Go, go, go! Hurry, Kate!
Hurry, Kate! You can't be late!

"Eat your breakfast! Brush your teeth!
The school bus doesn't wait!
Now it's 7:45,
And you can't be late!"

(Chorus)

Kate packs her backpack,
And she combs her hair.
Now it's 7:55,
And her bus is there!

(Chorus)

Kate gets on the bus, and then
She sees that something's wrong.
She gets to school on time that day
With her pajamas on!

(Chorus)

2 Listen. Look at the pictures. Point and say.

1. wake up

2. wash my face

3. eat breakfast

4. get dressed

5. brush my teeth

6. play soccer

7. play video games

8. do my homework

9. feed the cat

10. watch TV

3 Read and match.

1. 7:00	seven ten	**6.** 4:45	five twenty-five
2. 7:10	seven forty-five	**7.** 4:00	four forty-five
3. 7:30	seven fifty-five	**8.** 8:15	five thirty
4. 7:45	seven o'clock	**9.** 5:25	eight fifteen
5. 7:55	seven thirty	**10.** 5:30	four o'clock

4 Work with a partner. Listen. Look at the pictures. Ask and answer.

What time does she wake up?

She wakes up at seven o'clock in the morning.

What does he do at five thirty in the afternoon?

He feeds the cat.

Story

5 **Listen and read.**

1 Dylan wakes up and goes into the kitchen.

2 Before school, Dylan always eats breakfast.

3 He brushes his teeth. He washes his face.

4 He gets dressed.

4 Unit 1

5 He puts on his shoes. He's ready for school.

6 But there's no school today!

READING COMPREHENSION

6 Write *B* for *before school* or *A* for *after school.*

1. _____ Dylan eats breakfast.

2. _____ Dylan plays soccer.

3. _____ Dylan wakes up.

4. _____ Dylan brushes his teeth.

5. _____ Dylan washes his face.

6. _____ Dylan gets dressed.

7. _____ Dylan puts on his shoes.

8. _____ Dylan plays basketball.

7 THINK BIG Talk about the questions with a partner.

1. Why does Dylan like Mondays?

2. Why is Dylan surprised?

3. Do you like Mondays? Why or why not?

Language in Action

A8

8 **Listen and read. Say.**

Jenna: Hi, Ethan. Do you want to get together after school today?

Ethan: Sorry. I can't. I'm busy on Tuesdays.

Jenna: Really? What do you do?

Ethan: At 3:30, I have piano lessons. At 4:15, I go to soccer practice. Then I go home.

Jenna: Oh. What do you do after that?

Ethan: I do my homework, clean my room, and feed the dog. Then at 7:00, we eat dinner.

Jenna: Wow! You *are* busy.

9 **Look at pages 4 and 5. Ask and answer with a partner.**

What does Dylan do before school?

He wakes up, eats breakfast, . . .

A9

10 **Listen and stick. Number the pictures.**

What does he/she do **before** school?	He/She eats breakfast **before** school.
What do you do **after** school?	I play soccer **after** school.

11 **Look at Claudia's schedule. Write *before* or *after*.**

Claudia's Schedule	
6:30 wake up	**3:20** get home
6:45 get dressed	**3:30** ride my bike
7:00 eat breakfast	**4:45** do my homework
7:15 brush my teeth	**5:30** play soccer
7:30 go to school	**6:30** eat dinner

1. Claudia gets dressed ____before____ school.

2. Claudia does her homework _____ school.

3. Claudia brushes her teeth _____ school.

4. Claudia plays soccer _____ school.

5. Claudia eats breakfast _____ school.

12 **Read and match. Make sentences.**

_____ **1.** We eat breakfast at 7:30   **a.** at 5:00 in the afternoon.

_____ **2.** I wake up at   **b.** in the morning.

_____ **3.** Paula washes her   **c.** 8:00 in the evening.

_____ **4.** Tim does his homework at 4:15   **d.** face at 7:50 in the morning.

_____ **5.** Sandra plays video games   **e.** 6:45 in the morning.

_____ **6.** They watch TV at   **f.** in the afternoon.

13 **Look at 11. Talk about Claudia's schedule with a partner.**

Claudia wakes up at 6:30 in the morning.

She gets dressed at 6:45.

CONTENT WORDS

bacteria   cough   germs   healthy   sick   sneeze

A10

14 🎧 **Listen and read.**

Keep It Clean!

Washing your hands, showering, and brushing your teeth are three easy things you can do every day to keep yourself clean and healthy.

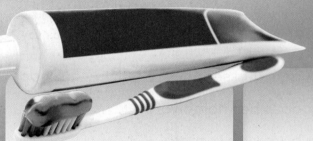

Take a Shower

When your parents tell you to take a shower, they are giving you good advice. Wash your face, behind your ears, and under your arms. Be sure to wash your whole body well. Use warm water and soap to wash away bacteria. Bacteria are tiny living things that can make you sick.

Brush Your Teeth

To keep your teeth strong and healthy, be sure to brush them twice a day. Brush in the morning when you wake up. And brush at night before you go to sleep. Brushing your teeth cleans away bacteria that can cause tooth decay. It's important to brush your teeth for at least two minutes at a time.

Wash Your Hands

Every day, our hands pick up millions of germs that can make us sick. Be sure to wash your hands with soap and water for at least twenty seconds. Wash your hands before you eat, after you visit the bathroom, after you cough or sneeze, and any other time your hands get dirty.

15 **Circle *T* for *true* or *F* for *false*.**

	True	False
1. Bacteria can make you sick.	T	F
2. Wash your hands only once a day.	T	F
3. Wash your hands after you take a shower.	T	F
4. Brush your teeth for at least two minutes at a time.	T	F
5. Brush your teeth five times a day.	T	F

16 Read and complete. Listen and check. A11

Time Zones

Do You Know What Time It Is?

Is it the same time everywhere in the world? No, it's not. That's because the world is divided into time zones. Look at the map of the United States. It has four different time zones.

	1:00 in the afternoon	two hours later	five more hours later
New York	It's 1:00 in New York, and Manuel and his friends are finishing their lunch.	Now it's ___:00 in New York, and school is over. Manuel is playing soccer.	It is ___:00 at night now in New York, and Manuel is finishing his homework.
Texas	In Texas, it's 12:00, and Maria is just finishing math class.	In Texas, it's ___:00, and Maria is still in school.	In Texas, it's ___:00, and Maria is eating dinner.
Montana	John, in Montana, is hungry and is thinking about lunch. He looks at the clock. It's only 11:00 in the morning!	It's ___:00 in Montana, and John is finishing his lunch.	In Montana, it's now ___:00, and John is making dinner with his dad.
California	And for Kara, in California, it's only 10:00 in the morning.	Kara, in California, looks at the clock, and it's ___:00. Hooray! It's lunchtime!	In California, Kara is playing with her sister. It's ___:00.

17 THINK BIG Work with a partner. Ask and answer.

1. When it's 6:00 p.m. in Montana, what time is it in California?

2. Manuel gets up at 7:00 in the morning. What is Kara doing when Manuel gets up?

3. How many time zones does your country have? Explain.

Unit 1 **9**

A sentence has a subject and a verb.
   She eats breakfast before school.
She is the subject. *Eats* is the verb.
   I ride my bike to school.
I is the subject. *Ride* is the verb.

18 **Read the sentences. Underline the subject. Circle the verb.**

1. Andrew eats breakfast at 7:30 in the morning.
2. Marcia goes to school at 8:05 in the morning.
3. We come home at 3:50 in the afternoon.
4. They do their homework at 4:30.
5. You eat dinner with your family in the evening.

19 **Complete the sentences with a subject or a verb. Use the words from the box.**

| brother | cleans | She | Tom | wakes |

1. Bridget _____ up at 6:45 in the morning.
2. _____ eats breakfast at 7:00.
3. Her _____ wakes up at 7:15 in the morning.
4. Bridget _____ her room before school.
5. _____ cleans his room after school.

20 **Write four sentences about your day. Read them to a partner.**

_____

_____

_____

_____

21 **Look and listen.**

I feed the dog
before school.

I clean my room
after school.

I wash the dishes
after dinner.

PROJECT

22 **What chores do you do at home? Add them to the chart. Check (✔).
Then ask three classmates about their chores.**

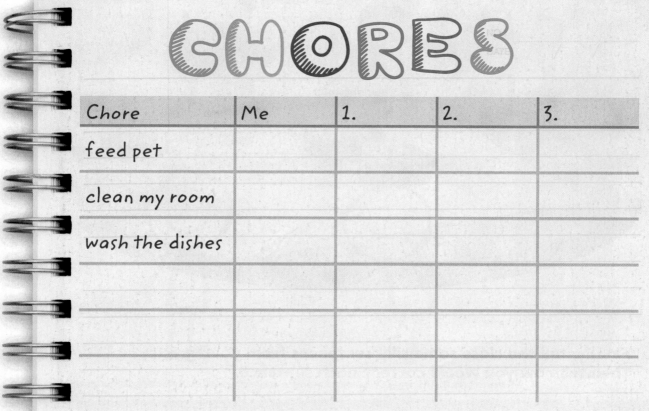

CHORES

Chore	Me	1.	2.	3.
feed pet				
clean my room				
wash the dishes				

23 Play the *Silly Sentences* game. First, write times on ten cards. Then write activities on ten cards.

Next, work in groups. Put the times cards in one stack and the activity cards in another. Shuffle the cards. Taking turns, choose a card from each stack and make a silly sentence.

Finally, tell the class some silly sentences from your group. Then tell how you would correct each sentence.

24 **Write three things you do in the morning, in the afternoon, and in the evening.**

Morning	Afternoon	Evening
1.	1.	1.
2.	2.	2.
3.	3.	3.

25 **Complete the paragraph. Use the words *after*, *at*, *before*, *in*, and *on*.**

    I like Fridays! Every Friday, I wake up ¹_____ 6:30 in the morning. I eat breakfast, brush my teeth, and get dressed. I always feed my cat ²_____ school. I like school ³_____ Fridays. We have art class, and I like to draw! At 3:45, I go to the park and play basketball with my friends. We always play sports ⁴_____ school. I go home at 5:30 ⁵_____ the afternoon, clean my room, and play video games. At 7:00, we eat pizza. We always have pizza for dinner on Fridays!

I Can ☐ say what I do before and after school.
         ☐ talk about different times of the day.

unit 2 In Our COMMUNITY

A13

1 Listen and read. Then sing.

Community Helpers

There are many people
In our community.
We all help each other.
Helping is the key!

Community helpers help us all—
Young, old, tall, and small.

Firefighters, farmers,
Chefs, and cashiers, too.
Doctors, nurses, barbers—
Just to name a few.

(Chorus)

People work in restaurants,
Hospitals, and stores,
Fire stations, laboratories,
Indoors and outdoors.

(Chorus)

So next time you go out,
Tell workers that you see,
"Thanks for everything you do
In our community!"

chef

firefighter

2 Listen. Point and say.

police officer

cashier

waiter

farmer

scientist

nurse

teacher

3 Listen and write. Say.

1. A _____nurse_____ works at a hospital.

2. A _____ works at a fire station.

3. A _____ works at a store.

4. A _____ works on a farm.

5. A _____ works at a police station.

6. A _____ works in a laboratory.

7. A _____ works at a school.

8. A _____ and a _____ work at a restaurant.

mail carrier

4 Work with a partner. Listen. Look at the pictures. Ask and answer.

Where do nurses work?

They work at a hospital.

Unit 2 **15**

A17–18

5 **Listen and read.**

Are You a Doctor?

1 A man is in a hospital.

Excuse me. Do you work at this hospital?

Yes, I do.

Oh, good. Can you help me?

Well, I . . .

2 He's looking for help.

You see, I have a terrible cold . . . *achoo!*

3 The man has a bad cold.

And I'm so hot . . .

Sir, I'm sorry, but . . .

4 The woman can't help the sick man

5 The man wants to find a doctor or a nurse.

6 The woman isn't a doctor or a nurse.

READING COMPREHENSION

6 Circle *T* for *true* and *F* for *false*.

	True	False
1. The man is sick.	T	F
2. The woman is a doctor.	T	F
3. The woman works at the hospital.	T	F
4. The man is a doctor.	T	F
5. The woman is a nurse.	T	F
6. The woman is a cashier.	T	F

7 **THINK BIG** Talk about the questions with a partner.

1. Who does the man think the woman is?

2. Does the woman help the man? Why or why not?

3. Do you ever go to a hospital? Explain.

Language in Action

 8 **Listen and read. Say.**

Emma: Where does your mom work?

Will: She works at a television station.

Emma: What does she do?

Will: She's a reporter.

Emma: That's really cool. I want to be a newspaper reporter someday. I love to write.

Will: You do? I don't. I want to be an artist. I love to draw!

 9 **Listen and stick. Number the pictures.**

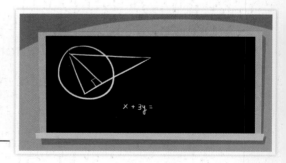

10 **Look at 9. Ask and answer questions with a partner.**

 What does he do?

He's a barber.

18 Unit 2

What **does** he/she **do**?	He/She **is** a nurse.
Where does he/she **work**?	He/She **works** at a hospital.
What **do** your sisters **do**?	They**'re** (They **are**) nurses.

11 **Complete the dialogues.**

1. **A:** What does your father _____do_____?

   B: He's a chef.

   A: Where _____ he work?

   B: He _____ at a restaurant.

2. **A:** What _____ your sisters Melanie and Patricia do?

   B: _____ firefighters.

   A: Where do they work?

   B: They _____ at a fire station.

12 **Number in order. Make a dialogue.**

__1__ **A:** What does your mom do?

_____ **B:** She works at a school.

_____ **A:** Where does she work?

_____ **B:** She's a nurse.

THINK BIG

13 **Ask and answer questions like the ones in 11.**

What does your dad do?

He's a farmer.

CONTENT WORDS

companies customers fashion designer professional storms video game

A27

14 Listen and read.

Unusual Jobs

There are many kinds of jobs in the world. Some are unusual! Would you like to do any of these jobs?

Video Game Tester

Ron Darley is a professional video game tester. He plays video games for eight hours a day. But it is not all fun—it's hard work. Ron must play each new game many times. If he finds a problem in a game, he writes it down. Companies use Ron's information to make the games better before customers buy them.

Storm Chaser

Mario Portillo is a storm chaser. He drives or flies near tornados, hurricanes, and other major storms. He observes their size, direction, and strength. Most storm chasers enjoy the thrill of being near storms. But their main purpose is to make videos of the storms. They sell the videos to websites and television news programs.

Doll Fashion Designer

Dana Forester is a fashion designer. But not for people—for dolls. Dana says, "Making clothes for dolls is fun. I get ideas from fashion shows, magazines, and catalogs. Then I create clothing that is 1/6 the size of a person. I'd like to make clothes for people someday. But for now, I'm happy trying out my ideas on dolls."

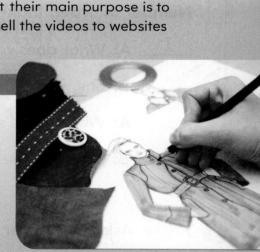

15 Correct the mistakes. Write the corrected sentences in your notebook.

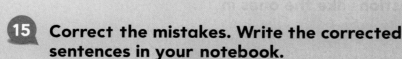

1. Mario Portillo is a weather reporter on TV.
2. Ron Darley plays video games for two hours each day.
3. Dana Forester designs clothes for children.

16 **Listen and read.**

Kids Working Hard

Here are three stories of kids working hard to make their communities better.

Lalana lives in Chiang Mai, Thailand. She knows that many schools in her city do not have money to buy books. Lalana and her friends ask people to donate books. They take the books to schools in their city. Many schools now have better books, thanks to Lalana and her friends.

Lalana

Carla lives in Barcelona, Spain. Many tourists visit Barcelona every year. Carla often sees people who are lost. On the weekends, Carla and her big sister help tourists find the places they are looking for. Carla likes helping people, and she's proud of her city.

Carla

Marcus lives in a small town near Melbourne, Australia. Marcus walks to school every day. He sees a lot of trash along the road. Marcus and his friends have a contest every day. They pick up the trash, and they see who can collect the most. They clean up the streets, and they have fun.

Marcus

17 **Circle _T_ for _true_ or _F_ for _false_.**

	True	False
1. Carla and her sister help tourists.	T	F
2. Lalana buys new books to give to schools.	T	F
3. Marcus takes a bus to school every day.	T	F
4. Marcus and his friends do not enjoy picking up trash.	T	F
5. Carla is proud of Barcelona.	T	F

A sentence can have a compound subject.
Al is a farmer. Pat is a farmer. → **Al and Pat are** farmer**s**.

A sentence can have a compound verb.
I live in Rome. I work in Rome. → I **live and work** in Rome.

18 **Rewrite the sentences. Use *and* to make a compound subject or verb.**

1. Lily is a scientist. Tom is a scientist.

   Lily and Tom are scientists.

2. My mother is a teacher. My father is a teacher.

   _____

3. I work at the restaurant. I eat at the restaurant.

   _____

4. My sister lives on a farm. My brother lives on a farm.

   _____

5. My grandfather lives in an apartment building. My grandfather works in an apartment building.

   _____

19 **Complete the sentences. Write about yourself.**

1. Before school I _____ and _____.

2. After school I _____ and _____.

3. _____ and I like to do things together after school.

20 Look and listen.

A23

21 Make a class book about respecting others.

22 Play the *Occupations* game. First, write an occupation on a sticky note. Don't show your partner.

Next, stick your partner's note to your forehead. Don't look! Ask questions. Guess the occupation.

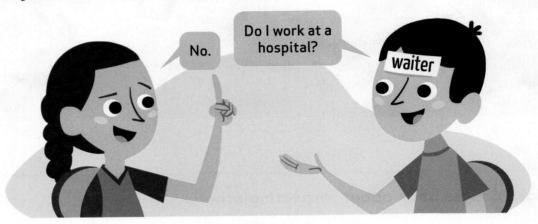

A: Do I work at a hospital?

B: No.

A: Do I work at a restaurant?

B: Yes.

A: Am I a chef?

B: No.

A: Am I a waiter?

B: Yes!

Finally, play the *Occupations* game with a group of classmates.

23 **Complete the dialogues.**

1. **A:** What do you _____?

   B: I'm a firefighter.

2. **A:** What does your brother do?

   B: He _____ a nurse.

3. **A:** What _____ your sister do?

   B: She's a scientist.

4. **A:** What do your parents do?

   B: They _____ teachers.

24 **Complete the sentences. Use the words from the box.**

cashier	farm	laboratory
nurse	police station	teacher

1. I'm a farmer. I work on a _____.

2. My brother is a _____. He works at a school.

3. My dad is a police officer. He works at a _____.

4. My grandmother is a _____. She works at a store.

5. My grandfather is a scientist. He works in a _____.

6. My uncle is a _____. He works at a hospital.

I Can ☐ **talk about what people do.**

☐ **talk about where people work.**

Working HARD

unit 3

A24

1 Listen and read. Then sing.

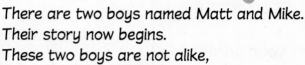

Different Twins

There are two boys named Matt and Mike.
Their story now begins.
These two boys are not alike,
Even though they're twins!

Mike and Matt. Matt and Mike.
These two twins are not alike.

Matt always cleans his room.
He does his chores each day.
He always studies for his tests.
He has no time to play.

(Chorus)

Mike never cleans his room.
He never makes his bed.
He never wants to play outside.
He watches TV instead.

(Chorus)

Which one are you like?
Are you like Mike or Matt?
You might be a bit like each.
There's nothing wrong with that!

2. Listen. Point and say.

1. I make my bed.

2. I walk the dog.

3. I practice the piano.

4. I take out the trash.

5. I wash the dishes.

6. I go to soccer practice.

7. I study.

8. I feed the cat.

3. Listen and say.

	Mon	Tue	Wed	Thu	Fri	Sat	Sun
1. I **always** make my bed.	✓	✓	✓	✓	✓	✓	✓
2. I **usually** make my bed.	✓		✓		✓	✓	✓
3. I **sometimes** make my bed.				✓			✓
4. I **never** make my bed.							

4. Complete the sentences. Use *always*, *never*, *sometimes*, and *usually*.

	Mon	Tue	Wed	Thu	Fri	Sat	Sun
1. He _____ washes the dishes.							
2. She _____ walks the dog.	✓	✓	✓		✓	✓	
3. They _____ feed the cat.	✓	✓	✓	✓	✓	✓	✓
4. She _____ makes her bed.	✓		✓			✓	

5. Work with a partner. Listen. Ask and answer questions.

Do you make your bed?

I usually make my bed. Sometimes I forget.

Story

6 **Listen and read.**

I Have a Lot to Do

Hey, Brenda . . .

Not now! I'm busy!

1 Brenda is thinking. Her sister comes in to her room.

Brenda, what are you doing?

Oh, sorry, Tina. I have a lot to do today. I'm making a list.

2 Brenda is making a list of things she has to do.

What do you have to do?

First, I have to eat breakfast, get dressed, and brush my teeth. Then I have to feed Hector, clean my room, and study for my math test.

3 Brenda has many things to do before school.

What time do you have to leave for school?

At 7:50. Why?

4 Brenda's clock says 7:15.

5 Brenda's clock isn't working.

6 Brenda doesn't want to be late for school.

7 **Read. Circle the correct word or words.**

1. Brenda has to do many things **before / after** school.

2. Brenda has to leave for school at **7:00 / 7:50**.

3. Brenda has to study for her **math / science** test.

4. Brenda **has to / doesn't have to** walk the dog.

5. Brenda **has to / doesn't have to** run to school.

8 **THINK BIG** **Talk about the questions with a partner.**

1. Why is Brenda making a list?

2. What happens to make Brenda late?

3. Are you ever late? Why or why not?

A30

9 Listen and read. Say.

Amy: Hey, Betsy, do you want to go skating after school today?

Betsy: Sorry, but I can't today. I have to go to my piano lesson.

Amy: Piano lesson?

Betsy: Uh-huh. I always have a piano lesson on Tuesday afternoons.

Amy: Oh, OK. How about tomorrow?

Betsy: Sure. Sounds great!

10 Practice the dialogue in 9 with a partner. Use the activities on pages 26–27.

A31

11 Listen and stick.

Monday	Tuesday	Wednesday	Thursday	Friday

What **does** he/she **have to** do?	He/She **has to** feed the dog.
What **do** you/we/they **have to** do?	I/We/They **have to** feed the dog.

12 **Complete the dialogues.**

1. **A:** What _____ you have to do in the morning?

   B: I _____ make my bed every morning.

2. **A:** What _____ Ted have to do after school?

   B: Ted _____ go shopping with his mom.

3. **A:** What _____ Camilla and Susie have to do this evening?

   B: They _____ study for a test.

I/You/We/They	always usually	wash the dishes.
He/She	sometimes never	takes out the trash.

13 **Look at the chart below. Write sentences about Leo.**

Leo's chores	Mon	Tue	Wed	Thu	Fri
makes his bed	✓		✓		
cleans his room	✓	✓	✓		✓
does his homework	✓	✓	✓	✓	✓
washes the dishes					

1. Leo sometimes makes his bed. _____

2. _____

3. _____

4. _____

14 **Work with a partner. Ask and answer questions about your chores.**

Do you always wash the dishes?

Yes, I always wash the dishes.

A32

15 **Listen and read.**

Weekly Allowance

Many kids around the world do chores to earn an allowance each week. Look at the list below. Each chore earns a certain amount. Let's say you want to earn ten U.S. dollars. Which chores would you do? How many times would you have to do each chore? Complete the chart.

Chore	Amount (in U.S. dollars)	Number of Times	Subtotal (in U.S. dollars)
wash the dishes	$0.25		
take out the trash	$0.25		
clean your room	$1.00		
sweep the floor	$0.50		
do laundry	$2.00		
make your bed	$0.25		
take care of the pets	$0.50		
help cook dinner	$1.00		
		TOTAL	

16 **Write sentences about yourself. Use *always*, *usually*, *sometimes*, or *never*.**

1. I take out the trash. _____

2. I clean my room. _____

3. I make my bed. _____

4. I wash the dishes. _____

A33

17 Listen and read.

Helping Out

All around the world, kids help out at home. Listen to some of these kids' stories. Would you like to have to do their chores?

Ivan

I live on a goat farm in France. We get milk from the goats to make cheese. My family sells the cheese, and I help take care of the goats. Every morning, I get up at 5 o'clock. I help my father feed the goats and get the milk. I go to school after I do my chores. It is hard work, but I like helping my dad.

Chen Wei

My mother makes the best noodles, and people come to her shop from all over Singapore to eat them. In the evening, her shop is very busy. So every day, after I do my homework, I help my mother cook noodles. We have fun cooking together. I love eating the noodles, too!

Leah

I live in Alaska. In the winter, it snows almost all the time. It is hard to walk on the sidewalks with so much snow on them. Everyone has to shovel snow. I shovel snow before I go to school every day. I don't mind—it's good exercise!

18 Circle *T* for *true* or *F* for *false*.

	True	False
1. Ivan's family makes cheese.	T	F
2. Alaska is a warm place.	T	F
3. Chen Wei doesn't eat noodles.	T	F
4. Ivan has to take care of the goats.	T	F
5. Leah has to shovel snow.	T	F

19 **THINK BIG** Talk about the questions with a partner.

1. Which child's chores would you prefer to do? Explain.

2. Which child's work seems difficult to you? Explain.

3. What are some good things about doing these chores?

Use capital letters for most words in titles.

Walter and the Squeaky Wheels

Don't capitalize the following words in titles:

- *a*, *an*, *the*   Taking Care of a Big Dog
- *at*, *for*, *in*, *on*, Good Things to Eat
  to, *with*
- *and*, *but*, *or*   My Brother and I

But if one of these words is first in a title, capitalize it.

The Big Blue Car
A Day at the Park with Grandma
To the Moon and Back

20 **Rewrite the titles. Use capital letters as needed.**

1. my sister's new job

   My Sister's New Job

2. too many chores for chester

   _____

3. helping out around the house

   _____

4. saving your allowance the easy way

   _____

5. the jobs kids like the best

   _____

6. helping my family is fun

   _____

7. fixing the car with my dad

   _____

21 Look and listen. Are they happy to help? Circle the happy face or the sad face.

Can you help me?

Sure!

Hey, I need some help!

Now? I'm watching TV.

1.

2.

Come help me, please.

OK. I'm coming, Grandma!

3.

22 Role-play the dialogues in **21** with a partner.

PROJECT

23 Make a sock puppet. With a partner, use your puppet to role-play helping someone.

Can you help me study for my spelling test?

Sure!

24 Check (✓) the boxes. Then complete the sentences with *always*, *usually*, *sometimes*, or *never*.

My Chores	Mon	Tue	Wed	Thu	Fri	Sat	Sun
1. I _____ clean my room.							
2. I _____ do my homework.							
3. I _____ wash the dishes.							
4. I _____ help my parents.							

Ask a partner about his/her chores. Fill in the chart.

Do you always wash the dishes?

No, I sometimes wash the dishes.

My Partner's Chores	Mon	Tue	Wed	Thu	Fri	Sat	Sun
1. He/She _____ cleans his/her room.							
2. He/She _____ does his/her homework.							
3. He/She _____ washes the dishes.							
4. He/She _____ helps his/her parents.							

Invite your partner to do something after school. Use your schedules.

Let's watch a movie on Tuesday after school.

Sorry, I have to study for a test on Tuesday.

How about Wednesday?

Sure!

25 **Complete the sentences. Use the words from the box.**

always   has to   have to   never   usually

1. Marissa _____ take her dog for a walk every afternoon.

2. Larry _____ helps his parents after school. He helps them every day.

3. Paolo _____ studies for his tests at home, but today he's studying at a friend's house.

4. Sammy and Todd _____ go to basketball practice at 4:00 today.

5. Leslie _____ makes her bed. Her mother is not happy!

26 **Number the sentences in the dialogue.**

_____ **A:** I can't tomorrow. I have to help my dad. How about Thursday?

_____ **B:** Sorry, I have to go to my piano lesson. How about tomorrow?

__1__ **A:** Let's play basketball after school today.

_____ **B:** Thursday? Yeah, Thursday is good. See you then.

I Can ☐ **talk about how often people do things.**
         ☐ **talk about what people have to do.**

How Well Do I Know It? Can I Use It?

1 **Think about it. Read and circle. Practice.**

😊 I know this.   😐 I need more practice.   🙁 I don't know this.

	PAGES			
Daily activities: eat breakfast, brush my teeth, practice the piano . . .	3, 27	😊	😐	🙁
Telling time: one o'clock, two thirty, 5:15 . . .	3	😊	😐	🙁
Occupations: cashier, firefighter, chef . . .	14–15	😊	😐	🙁
Workplaces: police station, restaurant, store . . .	15	😊	😐	🙁
What time does she take a shower? She takes a shower **at 7:00 in the morning.**	3	😊	😐	🙁
What does he do **before** school? He eats breakfast **before** school. What do you do **after** school? I watch TV **after** school.	6–7	😊	😐	🙁
What **does** he **do**? He **is** a cashier. Where **does** he **work**? He **works** at a store.	18–19	😊	😐	🙁
They **always** do their homework after school. She **usually** puts away the dishes. He **sometimes** takes out the trash. I **never** eat breakfast at 9:00.	27, 31	😊	😐	🙁
What **do** they **have to** do? They **have to** wash the dishes.	30–31	😊	😐	🙁

I Can Do It!

A35

2 **Get ready.**

A. Complete the interview. Use the questions from the box. Then listen and check.

> What do you do before work?
>
> Where do you work?
>
> Do you eat dinner at home?
>
> What time do you go to work?
>
> What do you do?

Katy: _____?

Max: I'm a chef.

Katy: Oh, really? _____?

Max: I work at a restaurant, the Pizza Palace.

Katy: I see. _____?

Max: I usually go to work at 2:00. I come home at 11:00 at night.

Katy: OK. _____?

Max: I take a shower, eat breakfast, and get dressed. Then I feed my cat.

Katy: _____?

Max: No, I always eat dinner at the restaurant.

B. Write more questions.

1. What time _____?
2. When _____?
3. _____ before work?
4. _____ in the afternoon?

C. Practice the dialogue in **A** with a partner. Include your new questions.

1

2

3

4

5

6

7

8

9

3 Get set.

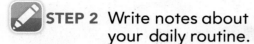 **STEP 1** Choose an occupation.

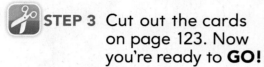 **STEP 2** Write notes about your daily routine.

STEP 3 Cut out the cards on page 123. Now you're ready to **GO!**

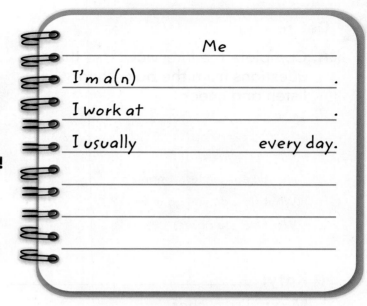

Me

I'm a(n) _____.

I work at _____.

I usually _____ every day.

4 Go!

A. Use the cards to make questions. Interview your partner. Write about your partner's daily routine. Then switch roles.

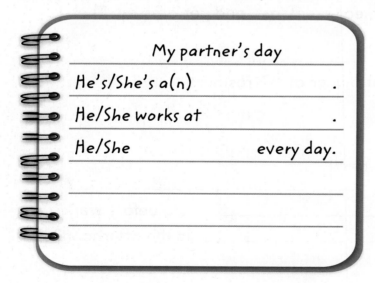

My partner's day

He's/She's a(n) _____ .

He/She works at _____ .

He/She _____ every day.

B. Work in groups. Tell your classmates about your partner's daily routine.

Luisa always eats breakfast before work.

5 Write about yourself.

- What time do you wake up?
- What do you do before school?
- What do you do after school?
- What time do you go to bed?

All About Me Date:_____

_____

_____

_____

_____

_____

How Well Do I Know It Now?

6 Think about it.

A. Go to page 38. Read and circle again. Use a different color.

B. Check (✔).

- ☐ I can start the next unit.
- ☐ I can ask my teacher for help and then start the next unit.
- ☐ I can practice and then start the next unit.
- ☐ _____.

7 Rate this Checkpoint. Color the stars.

☆ very easy ☆ easy ☆ hard ☆ very hard | ☆ fun ☆ not fun

unit 4 Awesome ANIMALS

A36

1 Listen and read. Then sing.

Animals Are Awesome!

Animals are awesome!
We see them far and near.
Some live in the forest—
Like owls, bears, and deer.

Some live in the desert—
Like camels and some snakes.
Some live in the water
In oceans, seas, and lakes.

Awesome, awesome animals—
What cool things you can do!
Awesome, awesome animals—
We share the Earth with you.

Sharks and other kinds of fish
Can swim in salty seas.
Parrots, ducks, and other birds
Can fly above the trees.

Sea lions and penguins
Can live in snow and ice.
Some animals are dangerous,
And some of them are nice!

(Chorus)

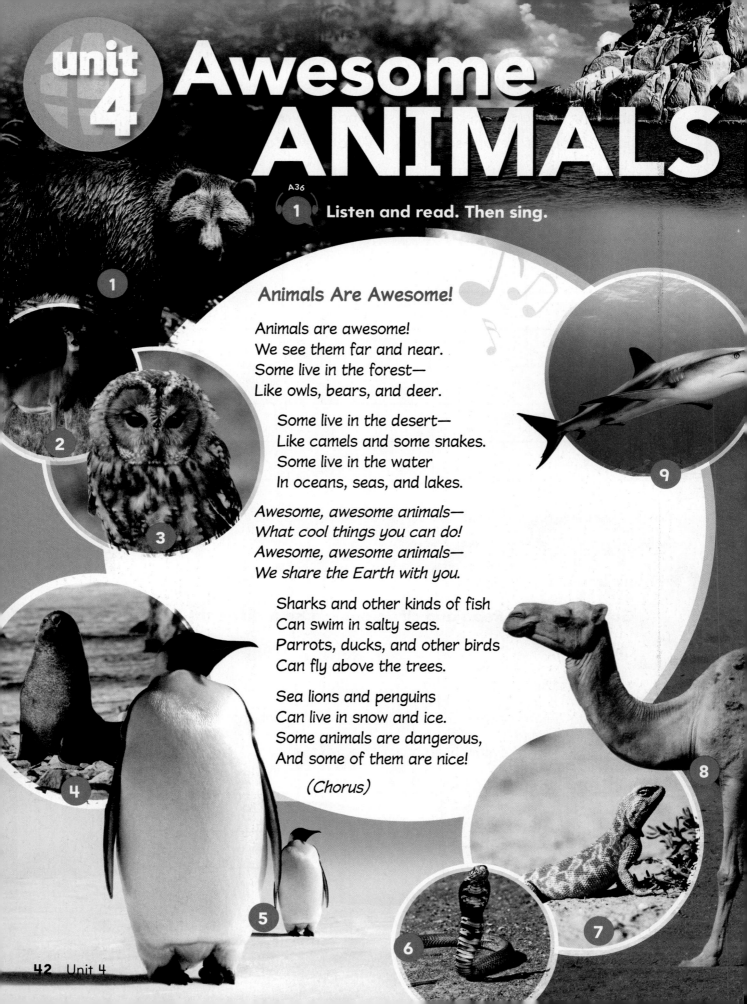

2 Listen. Point and say.

A37

1. bear	**4.** sea lion	**7.** lizard	**10.** fish
2. deer	**5.** penguin	**8.** camel	**11.** parrot
3. owl	**6.** snake	**9.** shark	**12.** duck

3 Look at the pictures. Which animals are your favorites? Ask and answer with a partner.

4 A38 **THINK BIG** Where do animals live? Work with a partner. Listen. Use the words from the box.

desert	forest
ice and snow	lake
ocean	rain forest

 Where do lizards live?

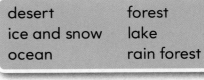 Some live in the desert, and some live in the rain forest.

Unit 4 **43**

5 Listen and read.

At the Zoo

Whoa! Kasey, look at that sea lion. It's clapping to the music!

CLAP! CLAP!

Oh, cool!

1 Kasey and Tyler are watching a sea lion show at the zoo.

Now it's trying to sing. What a bad sound!

Sea lions can't sing very well. But they are really cute!

2 The sea lion can't sing very well, and Tyler has to cover his ears.

Now it's balancing a ball!

Sea lions can do some great tricks!

3 The sea lion can balance a ball on its nose!

That parrot can ride a bike!

Awesome!

4 Then Tyler and Kasey watch a cute parrot show.

5 The parrot's name is Smartie.

6 When Smartie starts talking, she can't stop!

READING COMPREHENSION

6 **Read and match. Make sentences.**

_____ **1.** Sea lions can't

_____ **2.** Smartie is a

_____ **3.** Sea lions can

_____ **4.** Smartie can't

_____ **5.** Smartie can

a. stop talking.

b. do tricks.

c. sing very well.

d. parrot.

e. say her name.

7 **THINK BIG** **Talk about the questions with a partner.**

1. What are Tyler and Kasey doing at the zoo?

2. Do you think sea lions and parrots are intelligent? Why or why not?

3. Do you have a pet? If so, what can it do?

8 Listen and read. Say.

A41

Brad:	Are you ready for an animal quiz?
Samuel:	Yes, I am!
Brad:	OK. Listen. This animal lives in the ice and snow. It can swim, but it can't fly.
Samuel:	I know! It's a penguin.
Brad:	Right! Now it's your turn.
Samuel:	OK. Let's see . . . It lives in the forest. It can climb trees, and it can swim.
Brad:	Hmm . . . Is it a snake?
Samuel:	No. It has four legs, and it can run fast.
Brad:	Oh, I know. It's a bear!
Samuel:	That's right!

9 Listen and stick. Number the pictures.

A42

_____   _____   _____   _____

10 With a partner, talk about the animals on pages 42–43. Use *can* and *can't*.

 What can a fish do?

It can swim. It can't climb trees.

What **can** a penguin do?	It **can** swim. It **can't** fly.	subject + *can* / *can't* + verb
What **can** bears do?	They **can** climb. They **can't** fly.	
Can a penguin swim?	Yes, it **can**.	subject + *can* / *can't*
Can bears fly?	No, they **can't**.	

11 **Complete the sentences. Use *can* or *can't*.**

1. Ducks and sea lions _____ swim.

2. A shark _____ climb a tree.

3. A giraffe _____ reach the leaves at the top of a tree.

4. A penguin _____ fly, but an owl _____.

5. A parrot _____ talk, but a lizard _____.

12 **Look at pages 42–43. Write questions and answers. Add one of your own!**

1. Where do bears live? _____

2. Where do penguins live? _____

3. _____ They live in the ocean.

4. _____ They live in the rain forest.

5. _____

A43

13 **Listen and read.**

Animal Hide and Seek

Many animals blend in with their surroundings. This is called *camouflage*. Animals use color, body shape, or both to blend in. Camouflage helps animals hide and find food.

Chameleons Change Color

A chameleon can change its color. On a brown rock, it can be brown. In a green tree, it can be green. Very cool!

chameleon

Polar Bears Hide in the Snow

Polar bears live in the ice and snow. Everything around them is white. They are covered in white fur, except for their eyes, noses, and the bottoms of their feet. It's not easy to see a polar bear in the snow.

Animals Blend In for Different Purposes

The stonefish uses camouflage to get food. It looks like the stones on the sea floor. The fish it eats can't tell it apart from its surroundings. If they touch the stonefish by mistake, it stings them to death and eats them.

polar bear

The gray tree frog uses camouflage for protection. It looks like a tree branch. The birds and snakes that eat gray tree frogs can't see them against the bark of the tree.

Look at the pictures. Is it easy to see these animals?

stonefish

14 **Circle *T* for *true* or *F* for *false*.**

		True	False
1.	Animals can use color to hide.	T	F
2.	Chameleons can change color.	T	F
3.	Polar bears have white fur.	T	F
4.	The stonefish looks like tree bark.	T	F
5.	It is very easy for birds and snakes to see gray tree frogs.	T	F

gray tree frog

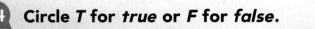

15 Listen and read.

Pets in Different Places

Many people around the world have pets. In the United States, Canada, and the United Kingdom, cats and dogs are very popular. In the United States, there are about 93 million pet cats and 77 million pet dogs.

Cats, dogs, and other animals are popular pets in other countries, too. In Japan, many people have a special kind of dog called a **shiba inu**. Dogs are also popular in China. But many people in China have goldfish as pets.

In Mexico, many people have cats and dogs. But birds such as parakeets are also popular. Parakeets are colorful, and they like to play with people. Some parakeets can even talk! In Italy, many people have canaries. Canaries can sing all day!

There are many different kinds of pets. Rabbits, hamsters, and snakes are also very popular around the world. What kind of pet do you like?

16 **THINK BIG** Ask and answer questions with a partner.

1. Do you have a pet? What kind? If not, what kind of pet do you want to have?

2. Which do you like better, cats or dogs? Why?

3. Do you think a snake is a good pet? Why or why not?

A topic sentence tells the main idea of a paragraph.
My favorite pet is my snake, Cornwall.

A45
17 **Listen and read.**

title →

My Favorite Pet
by Aaron Michaels

topic
sentence → My favorite pet is my snake, Cornwall.
He is a corn snake. He is 50 centimeters
(20 inches) long, and he is reddish brown with
black spots. I feed him one small mouse every
week. He eats very slowly. He is friendly. He
does not bite people. I like to hold him. Some
people don't like snakes, but snakes can make
good pets.

18 **Read and match the titles with the topic sentences.**

Title	Topic Sentence
_____ 1. A Day at the Zoo	**a.** My sister and I have many pets at home.
_____ 2. My Mother's Job	**b.** My favorite time of day at school is art class.
_____ 3. My Favorite Class	**c.** I have many jobs to do at home after school.
_____ 4. After-School Jobs	**d.** My mother is a chef at an Italian restaurant.
_____ 5. Our Pets	**e.** When I go to the zoo, I spend the whole day there.

19 **Write a title and a topic sentence for a paragraph
about your favorite pet or animal.**

_____

_____

_____

20 Look at the map of animals in South America.

Animals of South America

parrot
(rain forest)

bear
(forest)

snake
(rain forest)

mountain lion
(mountains)

We can protect the rain forest for the animals.

lizard
(rain forest)

penguin
(ice and snow)

21 **Work in a group. Make an Animals Map.**

- Choose a continent.
- Research the animals that live there.
- Draw and label your part of the map.

dingo
(grasslands)

koala
(forest)

kangaroo
(desert)

parrot
(rain forest)

kookaburra
(forest)

Animals of Australia

22 **Make an Animals quiz. Complete the questions with the names of ten different animals.**

Questions	Student 1: _____	Student 2: _____	Student 3: _____
1. Can a(n) _____ fly?	1.	1.	1.
2. Where does a(n) _____ live?	2.	2.	2.
3. Can a(n) _____ climb trees?	3.	3.	3.
4. Where does a(n) _____ live?	4.	4.	4.
5. Can a(n) _____ talk?	5.	5.	5.
6. Where does a(n) _____ live?	6.	6.	6.
7. Can a(n) _____ run fast?	7.	7.	7.
8. Where does a(n) _____ live?	8.	8.	8.
9. Can a(n) _____ swim?	9.	9.	9.
10. Where does a(n) _____ live?	10.	10.	10.

Write the answers to your questions below.

1. _____	3. _____	5. _____	7. _____	9. _____
2. _____	4. _____	6. _____	8. _____	10. _____

Ask three classmates your questions. Put a check (✓) next to correct answers. Put an X next to wrong answers.

Find out who got the highest number of correct answers.

23 **Think about the animals you know. Complete the chart.**

These animals can swim.	These animals can fly.
1.	1.
2.	2.
3.	3.
4.	4.

24 **Complete the dialogue.**

Daniel: Where do parrots live?

Teresa: _____.

Daniel: Right. _____

Teresa: Camels live in the desert.

Daniel: Right again! Can a camel run fast?

Teresa: _____.

Daniel: How about penguins? Can they fly?

Teresa: _____.
But they can swim.

Daniel: That's right!

I Can	☐ describe what animals can do.
	☐ describe what animals can't do.
	☐ say where animals live.

Sunny DAYS

1 Listen and read. Then sing.

A46

Boring Weekend

It was a boring weekend.
I really had no fun.
No bike, no park, no outdoor games—
There wasn't any sun!

I finished all my homework
And read a magazine.
I made my bed and cleaned my room.
It's never been so clean!

Rainy weekends are no fun.
What's a weekend without sun?

All weekend it was rainy,
Cold, and windy, too.
I did some chores and read a lot.
What else could I do?

Now it's Monday, and it's sunny.
It's a beautiful warm day.
Too bad I have to go to school!
I can't go out and play!

(Chorus)

2 **Listen. Point and say.**

1. It's cold and snowy.

2. It's warm.

3. It's cloudy and cool.

4. It's hot and sunny.

5. It's windy.

6. It's rainy.

3 **Listen. Write the number.**

sunglasses
shorts
sandals

sweater
scarf

raincoat
umbrella
boots

hat
coat
gloves

4 **Work with a partner. Listen. Ask and answer questions.**

What does he wear on hot, sunny days?

On hot, sunny days, he wears shorts, sandals, and sunglasses.

What do you wear on sunny days?

On sunny days, I wear a hat and sunglasses.

Story

5 🎧 **Listen and read.**

All Kinds of Weather

I'm ready for my hike. I have my hiking boots, water, and snacks.

1 Isabel is happy. Today her class is going on a hike.

Wait a minute. You need your raincoat and umbrella.

Why? Is it rainy?

2 Isabel's mother doesn't think Isabel is ready.

No, not right now. But yesterday it was rainy.

Oh . . .

3 She doesn't want Isabel to get wet.

And last night it was cold and windy. Take your hat and gloves, too.

OK . . .

4 She doesn't want Isabel to be cold.

5 Isabel tries to reassure her mom.

6 Now Isabel is ready for all kinds of weather!

READING COMPREHENSION

6 **Look at the story. Answer the questions with a partner.**

1. How was the weather the day before Isabel's hike?

2. How was the weather the night before the hike?

3. How is the weather on the day of the hike?

4. What is Isabel wearing on the day of the hike?

7 **THINK BIG Talk about the questions with a partner.**

1. Why does Isabel bring so many extra things on her hiking trip?

2. When do you wear a raincoat?

3. When do you wear a hat and gloves?

4. When do you wear sunglasses and sunscreen?

A52

8 Listen and read. Say.

Mom:	Eli, you can't go out dressed like that!
Eli:	But, Mom, it's not cold. It's just rainy.
Mom:	It's windy, too. I don't want you to get sick. Please wear your raincoat.
Eli:	Aww, Mom. I hate that raincoat.
Mom:	What's wrong with that raincoat?
Eli:	Everyone knows it was my sister's. I can't wear a girl's clothes.
Mom:	Wear it today, and you can get a new raincoat.
Eli:	A boy's raincoat?
Mom:	Yes.
Eli:	It's a deal.

9 Practice the dialogue in **8** with a partner.

A53

10 Listen and stick.

San Francisco	
Yesterday	Today

Puerto Rico	
Yesterday	Today

| How **is** the weather today? | It's hot and sunny. |
| How **was** the weather yesterday? | It **was** windy. Leaves **were** everywhere. |

11 **Look at the calendar. Write sentences about the weather.**

M	T	W	Th	F

1. Today is Friday. <u>It's sunny.</u>

2. Today is Monday. _____

3. Today is Tuesday. _____

4. Today is Wednesday. _____

5. Today is Thursday. _____

12 **Complete the dialogue.**

A: Yesterday was great. We _____ at the beach all day.

B: How _____ the weather?

A: It _____ warm. How _____ the weather today?

B: It _____ rainy and cool. We can't go to the beach today.

Yesterday

Today

13 **How's the weather? Ask and answer questions with a partner.**

How's the weather today?

It's sunny and cool.

CONTENT WORDS

average   climate   extreme   opposite   temperature   tourists

A54

14 **Listen and read.**

How's the Weather?

The year-round weather in a place is called its *climate*. In some places, the climate is the same all year long—and it can be extreme.

Wow! That's Hot!

There are many hot places on the planet, but the Lut Desert in Iran is super hot. The temperatures there can reach 70 degrees Celsius (159 degrees Fahrenheit)! It is so hot that not many people go there. As a result, the Lut Desert is also a very quiet place.

It's Freezing!

Oymyakon, Russia, is the opposite of the Lut Desert. It is very cold. There is lots of snow, and temperatures can reach −70 degrees Celsius (−95 degrees Fahrenheit). But the cold weather doesn't stop people from living in Oymyakon. About 800 people live there.

I'm Thirsty!

The Atacama Desert in Chile is dry. In some parts of this desert, it never rains at all. Not many people live there, but tourists go to see this very beautiful place. People say the Atacama Desert looks like the moon.

Where's My Umbrella?

It rains almost every day in Lloró, Colombia. Lloró gets an average of 13 meters (40 feet) of rain every year. That's a lot of rain! But the people there don't mind. They earn money by cutting down trees in the forest. The trees grow back quickly because of the unusually rainy climate.

15 **Label the places with the correct word: *hot*, *cold*, *dry*, or *wet*.**

1. Lloró, Colombia _____
2. Lut Desert, Iran _____
3. Oymyakon, Russia _____
4. Atacama Desert, Chile _____

16 **What's the climate like where you live? Explain.**

_____

17 Listen and read.

All-Weather Sports

Children around the world enjoy outdoor sports. In the United States, many children play baseball. In India, cricket is a popular game. And soccer is loved by children all over the world. But when the weather is bad, it's not much fun to play any of these sports. So what can you do? Kids in other parts of the world just might have the answer.

Flying High

If it's too windy, it can be difficult to play soccer and some other outdoor sports. But one thing many kids know is that a windy day is great for flying a kite. Children all over the world enjoy being outdoors and flying kites.

Fun in the Water

In parts of Africa, it is dry for many months of the year. But when the rain comes, the dry rivers and lakes fill up quickly. Kids love it. They go swimming and play games in the water. It is a happy time for everyone when it rains.

Sledding

In Alaska and parts of Canada and the northern United States, it snows a lot. But that doesn't stop kids from having fun outdoors. When it snows, they dress in warm clothes and go outside. They often go sledding. Some kids also do an interesting sport called dog sledding. Dogs pull the sled, and the kids ride on it.

So turn off the TV. Even if it is windy, wet, or cold, there are lots of fun things to do outside.

18 THINK **BIG** Work with a partner. Ask and answer.

1. What do you like to do when it's cold out?
2. What do you like to do when it's really hot out?
3. What is your favorite weather? What do you like to do on those days?

Here is a topic sentence.

My favorite season is summer.

After the topic sentence, give more information. Write detail sentences.

In the summer where I live, the weather is usually sunny and hot. I like to go to the beach with my friends. We swim or play volleyball. We have fun.

A56

19 **Listen and say the words.**

spring   summer   fall   winter

20 **Read the topic sentence below. Which sentences give details about this topic? Check (✓) them.**

Topic sentence: *Winter is my favorite time of year.*

☐ **1.** It is cold and snowy in winter, but I like it.

☐ **2.** It is not cold in summer.

☐ **3.** My friends and I like to go sledding.

☐ **4.** We usually wear hats and gloves in winter.

☐ **5.** My sister's favorite season is spring.

☐ **6.** We like to build snowmen in winter, too.

21 **Write a topic sentence about your favorite season. Write three detail sentences under it.**

Topic sentence: _____

_____

Detail sentences: **1.** _____

2. _____

3. _____

22 Look and listen. Number the pictures.

A57

23 Work with a group. Make a Prepare for the Weather checklist.

Prepare for the Weather

sunscreen ☐   gloves ☐

sunglasses ☐   hat ☐

water ☐   umbrella ☐

24 **THINK BIG** Find the differences between the two pictures. Talk about the differences with a partner and make a list.

 In Picture A, it's hot and sunny.

In Picture B, it's cold and snowy.

Picture A

Picture B

Compare lists with other students in your class. Make one list for the whole class.

25 **Look at the weather reports. Complete the sentences.**

Santo Domingo, Dominican Republic	
Yesterday	Today
Temperature: 33° C / 91° F	Temperature: 28° C / 82° F

Vancouver, Canada	
Yesterday	Today
Temperature: 4° C / 39° F	Temperature: 12° C / 54° F

1. Yesterday in Santo Domingo, it was hot and _____ with a temperature of 33 degrees Celsius.

2. Today in Santo Domingo it is _____ and warm with a temperature of 28 degrees Celsius.

3. Yesterday in Vancouver it was cold and _____ with a temperature of 4 degrees Celsius.

4. Today in Vancouver it is _____ and cool with a temperature of 12 degrees Celsius.

26 **Complete the dialogue. Use a form of the verb *be*.**

Mom: What's wrong? Why are your clothes wet?

Haley: Adela and I _____ outside.

Mom: But it _____ sunny and beautiful outside!

Adela: No. It _____ sunny this morning.

Haley: Now it _____ rainy.

Mom: Oh, no!

I Can
- ☐ talk about the weather.
- ☐ say how the weather was yesterday.
- ☐ say what I wear in different kinds of weather.

B1
1 Listen and read. Then sing.

Grandma's House

I love to visit Grandma's house.
It always smells so nice.
It smells like ginger cookies—
Sweet, with a little spice!

Grandma smiles at me and says,
"I'm so glad you're here!"
Then she hugs and kisses me,
And calls me names like "Dear."

Yummy smells and her smiling face.
I really love my grandma's place.

Grandma likes to play old songs
From times when she was young.
The music sounds so wonderful,
I have to sing along.

We always do my favorite thing—
Walking Mr. Chettham.
This dog looks cute and friendly,
So people stop to pet him.

(Chorus)

2 Listen. Draw a happy or sad face in the box.

1. This music sounds pretty.

2. This soup tastes awful.

3. This pie tastes delicious.

4. These flowers smell nice.

5. My hair looks terrible.

6. My sweater feels soft.

7. These shoes feel tight.

8. This apple tastes sweet.

9. The band sounds bad.

3 Under each picture, write the word *feels*, *looks*, *smells*, *sounds*, or *tastes*.

1. _____ 2. _____ 3. _____ 4. _____ 5. _____

4 Work with a partner. Ask and answer.

How does the pie taste?

It tastes good.

Story

5 Listen and read.

How Does It Taste?

Ewww! . . . What's that smell?

What smell?

1 Greg smells something bad coming from the kitchen.

Yuck. This soup doesn't look good. Here . . . try it, Maddie!

OK.

2 It is fish soup.

How does it taste?

It tastes . . . OK.

3 Maddie tries the soup.

Let me try it.

4 Greg can't believe it. Maybe the soup tastes good!

5 Greg thinks the soup tastes awful.

6 Maddie has a cold. That's why she doesn't think the soup tastes bad.

Yuck! It tastes terrible!

Sorry. I have a cold. . . . Achoo! . . . I can't smell or taste anything.

READING COMPREHENSION

6 **Write numbers to put the sentences in order.**

_____ Maddie thinks the soup tastes OK.

_____ Greg thinks the soup tastes terrible.

_____ Greg thinks the fish soup smells bad.

_____ Maddie tries the soup.

_____ Greg tries the soup.

_____ Greg asks his sister Maddie to try the soup.

THINK
7 **BIG** **Work with a partner. Ask and answer.**

1. Why doesn't Greg like the soup?

2. Why can't Maddie taste the soup?

3. What foods taste bad to you? Explain.

Language in Action

8 Listen and read. Say.

Cindy: Hey, Mark. Do you want to hear my new song?

Mark: Uh . . . OK. Sure.

Cindy: *I don't want to run or play.*
I just want to sing all day.
So, how does it sound?

Mark: Um . . . it sounds . . . nice.

Cindy: Thanks! Do you want to hear more?

Mark: Uh . . . sorry, Cindy. I have to go.
See you later!

9 Practice the dialogue in **8** with a partner.

10 Listen and stick. Number the pictures.

| How **does** the apple pie **taste**? | It **tastes** delicious. |
| How **do** your new shoes **feel**? | They **feel** good. |

11 **Circle the correct verb.**

1. A: How does the school band **sound / sounds**?

   B: They **sound / sounds** great. They practice every day.

2. A: How does my new shirt **look / looks**?

   B: It **look / looks** good. I like the color.

3. A: How does the sandwich **taste / tastes**?

   B: It **taste / tastes** awful. I don't like tomatoes!

4. A: How do these flowers **smell / smells**?

   B: They **smell / smells** nice.

5. A: How do your new gloves **feel / feels**?

   B: They **feel / feels** really warm.

12 **Complete the questions with *do* or *does*.**

1. How _____ that pizza taste?

2. How _____ the cookies smell?

3. How _____ my hair look today?

4. How _____ the shoes feel?

5. How _____ the guitar music sound?

13 **THINK BIG** Work with a partner. Ask and answer questions. Use the topics in **2**, on page 67.

How does the music sound?

It sounds pretty.

CONTENT WORDS

avoid brain danger echo information tongues

B8

14 Listen and read.

Our Senses Keep Us Safe

Every minute of every day, our senses take in information and send it to the brain. We use this information to understand the world around us. Our senses tell us whether food is fresh or rotten and whether something is hot or cold. Our senses help keep us safe.

Like people, animals use their senses to find food and avoid danger. But many animals' senses are different from people's senses.

Did You Know?

■ Some animals, such as snakes and lizards, don't smell with their noses. They smell with their tongues!

■ Chameleons have very long, sticky tongues. They use their tongues to catch their food and to taste it!

■ Butterflies and some other insects taste things with their legs.

■ Bats' eyes cannot see well. To "see" things, they make a sound and listen for the echo. They can use their hearing to "see" how big something is and find it.

15 Read and match. Make sentences.

_____ 1. Butterflies taste

_____ 2. People and animals

_____ 3. Snakes and lizards

_____ 4. Bats use their

a. need their senses to be safe.

b. smell with their tongues.

c. ears to "see" things.

d. with their legs.

B9
16 Listen and read.

How Does Your Job Smell?

André Tyrode

I live in Lyon, France. I'm a baker. I get up early every day and make pastries. Of course, everything I make tastes good. But the bakery smells wonderful! It makes people want to sit and share delicious treats together. And that makes me happy.

Alberto Rivera

I'm from Costa Rica. I grow flowers on my farm. I sell them and send them all over the world. I like my job because I can look at flowers and smell them all day!

Candace Reilly

I'm from Calgary, a city in Alberta, Canada. My job is very important. I pick up trash and help keep my city clean. Today, Calgary is the cleanest city in Canada! My job doesn't smell great, but I like it.

Sarah Ang

I work at the Singapore Zoo, one of the best zoos in the world. This is Zelda. She is an Asian elephant. I take care of Zelda at the zoo. Sometimes Zelda doesn't smell very good, so I give her a bath! I like taking care of animals.

17 **THINK BIG** **Work with a partner. Ask and answer.**

1. Which job sounds interesting to you? Why?

2. Would you like to have any of these jobs in the future? Why or why not?

3. What jobs in your country involve good or bad smells? Explain.

As you know, a paragraph begins with a topic sentence. It introduces the subject of the paragraph.

I love tomatoes.

Detail sentences expand on your topic by giving details about it.

Home-grown tomatoes taste delicious, and they are good for you.
Fresh tomatoes right from the garden smell great.
They look nice in a salad, too.

You end your paragraph with a final sentence. It expresses the same idea as your topic sentence but in a different way.

Of all fruits and vegetables, tomatoes are my favorite.

18 **Read the paragraphs. Check (✓) the best final sentence for each.**

1. Topic Sentence: My favorite toy is my teddy bear, Simpson.

Detail Sentences: Simpson is very old. He doesn't look very nice. But I like him very much. He feels soft, and he always smells so nice. Simpson can't talk. Simpson can't run. But that's OK!

Final Sentence: ☐ **a.** Simpson is just an old teddy bear.

☐ **b.** I love Simpson more than any of my other toys.

☐ **c.** Simpson doesn't do anything.

2. Topic Sentence: My favorite teacher is Mrs. Graham.

Detail Sentences: Mrs. Graham is very nice. She teaches us many interesting things. Mrs. Graham never gets angry. Mrs. Graham is friendly, and she smiles a lot.

Final Sentence: ☐ **a.** Mrs. Graham is 40 years old.

☐ **b.** Mrs. Graham doesn't like cake very much.

☐ **c.** Mrs. Graham is the best teacher at our school.

19 **Write a final sentence for this paragraph:**

Fall is my favorite season. The colorful leaves on the trees look so pretty. The air feels nice and cool. And fall smells great—like pumpkins and burning leaves.

Final Sentence: _____

_____

20 Look and listen. Number the pictures.

_____   _____   _____

21 THINK **BIG** Practice with a partner. Talk about something new that you want to try.

My mom showed me how to make oatmeal cookies. Do you want to make them with me?

OK!

22 Work with a group. Make a Try New Things flip chart.

Try New Things

bake cookies

23 Complete the sentences with your own information.

1. My school lunch tastes _____.

2. When I sing, I sound _____.

3. My dog smells _____.

4. My _____ always helps me at home.

5. On the teacher's desk, I can see a(n) _____.

6. I want to have a pet _____ at home.

24 Write your answers from **23** next to the correct numbers in the dialogue. Practice the dialogue with one or more partners.

Troy: Hi, Daniela.

Daniela: Hi, Troy. Is that a new ⁵_____?

Troy: Yes, it is.

Daniela: It looks ²_____.

Troy: It's a present from my ⁴_____. Hey, what are you eating?

Daniela: Oh, that's my lunch. It's a ⁶_____ sandwich.

Troy: Hmm . . . OK. It smells ³_____.

Daniela: I know. It tastes ¹_____, too!

Troy: See you later.

Daniela: Bye!

25 **Look at the pictures. Complete the questions.**

1. How does the ice cream _____?

2. How does the rock band _____?

3. How does the woman _____?

4. How does the stuffed animal _____?

5. How do the flowers _____?

26 **Write answers to the questions in 25.**

1. _____

2. _____

3. _____

4. _____

5. _____

I Can ☐ **describe things by telling how they look, feel, taste, smell, or sound.**

☐ **talk about the five senses.**

Checkpoint | Units 4–6

How Well Do I Know It? Can I Use It?

1 **Think about it. Read and circle. Practice**

😊 I know this.   😐 I need more practice.   😟 I don't know this.

	PAGES			
Animals: deer, owl, camel, lizard . . .	42–43	😊	😐	😟
Habitats: desert, ocean, forest . . .	43	😊	😐	😟
Weather: hot, cold, windy, rainy . . .	55	😊	😐	😟
Describing: awful, delicious, nice, pretty, soft, tight . . .	67	😊	😐	😟
What **can** a penguin do? It **can** swim. It **can't** fly. **Can** bears fly? No, they **can't.**	46–47	😊	😐	😟
How **is** the weather today? **It's** hot and sunny. How **was** the weather yesterday? It **was** windy. Leaves **were** everywhere, and we **were** cold!	55, 58–59	😊	😐	😟
How **does** the apple pie **taste**? It **tastes** delicious. How **do** your new shoes **feel**? They **feel** good.	70–71	😊	😐	😟

I Can Do It!

B11

2 **Get ready.**

A. Complete the dialogue. Use the words from the box. Then listen and check.

> awful   cold   fly
> look   swim

Morgan: Look at those penguins!

Taylor: They _____ cool!

Morgan: Yeah. I like penguins. Hey, look at this: "Penguins live in the snow and ice."

Taylor: That sounds _____!

Morgan: Yes, very cold. Listen. "They eat fish every day." Look. They're eating fish now!

Taylor: Yuck! That looks _____ to me!

Morgan: Well, the penguins like it.

Taylor: Hey, look. They're swimming.

Morgan: Yes, penguins can _____. But they can't _____.

Taylor: Wow. I'm learning a lot about penguins!

B. Practice the dialogue in **A** with a partner. Then practice again. Talk about different animals.

C. Circle the word(s) that tell what YOU think.
  1. I **like / don't like** penguins.
  2. Their food looks **delicious / terrible** to me.
  3. Their home looks **warm / cold** to me.

3 **Get set.**

STEP 1 Look and read. Find out information about an animal.

STEP 2 Cut out the book outline on page 125. Fold it to make a book.

STEP 3 Create your own animal information book. Now you're ready to **Go!**

4 **Go!**

A. Trade books with five classmates. Write notes about your classmates' books.

Classmate	Animal	Comment
Carla	lizards	awesome

B. Tell the class about some of your classmates' books.

> Abby's book was about sharks. Sharks are amazing!

5 Write about yourself.

- How is the weather today?
- How was the weather yesterday?
- Today I can . . .
- Today I can't . . .

- Today the sky looks . . .
- My classroom feels . . .
- My favorite animal is . . .
- I like this animal because . . .

All About Me   Date:_____

_____

_____

_____

_____

_____

How Well Do I Know It Now?

6 Think about it.

A. Go to page 78. Read and circle again. Use a different color.

B. Check (✔).

☐ I can start the next unit.

☐ I can ask my teacher for help and then start the next unit.

☐ I can practice and then start the next unit.

7 Rate this Checkpoint. Color the stars.

☆ very easy   ☆ easy   ☆ hard   ☆ very hard | ☆ fun   ☆ not fun

1

2

3

4

5

6

7

8

9

unit 7 Fabulous FOOD

1 **Listen and read. Then sing.**

Hungry After School

"Hey, Mom, I'm home from school.
I'm really hungry now.
I want to make a sandwich,
But I don't know how.

*I am home from my school day.
I need a sandwich right away!"*

Mom says, "You can do it.
It's easy. It's a breeze!
Get some ham and lettuce.
    Get yourself some cheese."

(Chorus)

"Are there any tomatoes?
Here are some on the shelf.
Is there any mustard?
I see it for myself."

(Chorus)

"There's just one little problem, Mom—
There isn't any bread!
But I have a great idea:
Let's have pizza instead!"

(Chorus)

B13

2 Listen. Point and say.

1. pizza

2. tomato sauce   3. cheese   4. green peppers

5. onions   6. mushrooms   7. sausage   8. pepperoni

9. sandwich   10. bread   11. ham   12. pickles

13. lettuce   14. tomatoes   15. mustard   16. ketchup

3 **THINK BIG** Talk about the questions with a partner.

1. Which food looks good to you? Why?
2. What kind of pizza do you like?
3. What sandwiches do you like?

B14

4 Work with a partner. Listen. Ask and answer.

What kind of pizza do you like?

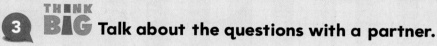

I like pizza with cheese and mushrooms.

Story

B15–16

5 **Listen and read.**

A Surprise for Mom

Are there any tomatoes for the pizza?

I don't see any tomatoes, but here's some cheese.

1 Lucy and Luke are making dinner for their mother. It's a surprise.

Are there any onions?

There aren't any onions, but there's one green pepper. And some mushrooms.

2 The children need toppings for their pizza.

This cheese is yummy.

Mmm. These mushrooms are delicious, too.

3 Lucy and Luke taste some of the pizza toppings.

Oh, no! There's no more cheese!

And there are no more mushrooms! What can we make for Mom now?

4 They eat all the cheese and the mushrooms.

Lucy and Luke take more food out of the refrigerator.

There's a surprise for Mom in the kitchen, but it isn't dinner!

READING COMPREHENSION

6 **Circle _T_ for _true_ and _F_ for _false_.**

		True	False
1.	Lucy and Luke want to make dinner for their mother.	T	F
2.	There aren't any onions for a pizza topping.	T	F
3.	Lucy and Luke eat all the cheese and mushrooms.	T	F
4.	Lucy and Luke make a fruit salad for their mother.	T	F
5.	Mom's surprise is an empty refrigerator and a messy kitchen.	T	F

7 **THINK BIG** **Talk about the questions with partner.**

1. What do you think Lucy and Luke's mom does next?
2. Do you like to surprise your parents? Explain.

8 **Listen and read. Say.**

B17

Felipa: What are you making, Mom?

Mom: I'm making some salsa.

Felipa: That sounds great!

Mom: I have some tomatoes, some chili peppers. . . . Are there any onions over there?

Felipa: Yes. Here they are.

Mom: Thanks.

Felipa: Mmm. That looks delicious, Mom. But there's a little problem.

Mom: What?

Felipa: Now we have salsa, but there aren't any chips!

9 **Practice the dialogue in 8 with a partner.**

10 **Listen and stick. Number the pictures.**

B18

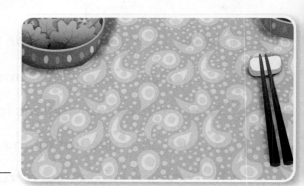

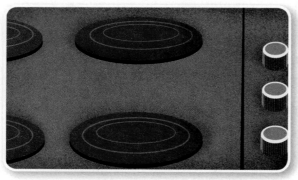

| Is there **any** pizza? | Yes, there is **some** pizza. | Are there **any** onions? | Yes, there are **some** onions. |
| Is there **any** fish? | No, there isn't **any** fish. | Are there **any** eggs? | No, there aren't **any** eggs. |

11 **Look at the chart above. Circle the correct word.**
1. There are (some) / any apples on the table.
2. There aren't **some / any** eggs in the refrigerator.
3. There isn't **some / any** milk in the carton.
4. There are **some / any** pickles in the jar.
5. There aren't **some / any** onions in this stew.

12 **Look at pages 82 and 83. Write questions and answers.**

1. Is there any cheese? _____

2. Are there any onions? _____

3. _____
No, there isn't any cake.

4. _____
No, there aren't any bananas.

5. _____
Yes, there are some tomatoes.

CONTENT WORDS

blood	bone	energy
remember	vegetables	vitamin

B19

13 🎧 **Listen and read.**

The Vitamin Alphabet

Vitamins help our bodies grow strong and stay healthy. We need vitamins every day. How do we get them? Just remember the vitamin alphabet: A, B, C, D, E.

	What It Does	Where We Get It
Vitamin A	Vitamin A is good for our eyes and skin. It helps them stay healthy.	Vitamin A is in carrots, mangoes, milk, and eggs.
Vitamin B	There are many different kinds of Vitamin B: Vitamin B1, B2, B6, B9, and B12. Some help give us energy. Others help make blood.	Vitamin B is in potatoes, bananas, bread, rice, pasta, chicken, fish, cheese, eggs, and green vegetables.
Vitamin C	Vitamin C is good for our bones, teeth, and even our brains.	We get Vitamin C from oranges, peppers, tomatoes, and potatoes.
Vitamin D	Vitamin D helps make strong bones.	We get Vitamin D from eggs, fish, milk—and from the sun, too!
Vitamin E	Vitamin E helps keep our blood healthy.	Vitamin E is in nuts and green vegetables.

14 💬 **Look at the chart. Write the answers in your notebook.**

1. Which vitamins help our bones?
2. How many different kinds of Vitamin B are in the chart?
3. Which vitamin do we get from the sun?

15 **Listen and read.**

Breakfast in Different Countries

Breakfast is a great way to start the day. Kids around the world eat many different things for breakfast. Here are just a few examples:

Japan

My name is Yoko. I'm from Japan. In the morning, I usually eat rice, soup, fish, and pickles. But sometimes I eat toast and eggs.

Spain

I'm Luis, and I'm from Spain. I usually eat bread or cereal for breakfast. But sometimes I drink hot chocolate and eat *churros*—they're like little donuts. They're delicious!

Mexico

My name is Camila. I'm from Mexico. For breakfast, I often eat *huevos rancheros*—fried eggs on toasted tortillas with *pico de gallo*, or salsa. Huevos rancheros are spicy and colorful and delicious!

Australia

My name's Tony. I live in Australia. I like to eat toast in the morning— with beans on top! Yum!

16 **THINK BIG** **Talk about the questions with a partner.**

1. What do you eat for breakfast?

2. Do you eat the same food for breakfast every day? Why or why not?

3. Which of these breakfast foods look good to you? Why?

B21

 17 **Listen and read.**

title ⟶

My Favorite Breakfast
by Laura Brown

topic
sentence ⟶

> I like many foods for breakfast, but I have my favorite breakfast every Sunday morning.

detail
sentences ⟶

> I start with some orange slices, cold from the refrigerator. Then my mother makes two fluffy pancakes for me. I put butter on them, and then I put warm maple syrup on top. The pancakes are delicious with a glass of cold milk.

final
sentence ⟶

> My favorite breakfast makes Sundays special.

B21

18 **Listen to Laura's paragraph again. Work with a partner. Take turns and read each part of the paragraph aloud.**

19 **Write about your favorite meal.**

_____

(title)

_____

_____

_____

_____

_____

_____

_____

Writing Steps

1. Think about your favorite meal.

2. Write a title.

3. Write a topic sentence.

4. Add detail sentences to give more information.

5. Write a final sentence.

20 **Listen. Look at the poster.**

Peruvians love potatoes. Peru grows more than 2,300 types of potatoes. There are many different shapes, sizes, and colors!

Potatoes grow very well in the cool weather, high in the Andes Mountains.

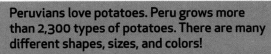
Potatoes in Peru

The most famous dish is *papa a la huancaína*—potatoes in a spicy cheese sauce.

Another is *papa rellena*, or stuffed potato. This dish has meat, onions, and eggs stuffed inside a potato.

Which dish looks good to you? Tell a partner.

I want to try the stuffed potato. It looks delicious!

PROJECT

21 **Make a poster about the food in a country other than your own.**

1. Learn about the typical foods in that country
2. Cut out pictures of the foods.
3. Label the pictures.
4. Share your poster with the class.

CHINA

noodles

dumplings

fried rice

22 **Make up a sandwich with five items.**

My sandwich has bread and...
1.
2.
3.
4.
5.

Ask other classmates about their sandwiches.

Is there any cheese on your sandwich?

Are there any tomatoes on your sandwich?

No, there isn't.

Yes, there are.

Make notes about your classmates' sandwiches. Try to find two people with the same sandwich.

Student 1: _____	Student 2: _____	Student 3: _____
1.	1.	1.
2.	2.	2.
3.	3.	3.
4.	4.	4.
5.	5.	5.

23 Look at the chart below. Write **S** for *sandwich item*, **P** for *pizza topping*, or **B** for *both*.

1. ___ lettuce	5. ___ mushrooms	9. ___ pepperoni	13. ___ ham
2. ___ bread	6. ___ sausage	10. ___ ketchup	14. ___ pickles
3. ___ tomato sauce	7. ___ green peppers	11. ___ cheese	15. ___ tomatoes
4. ___ onions	8. ___ mustard	12. ___ chicken	16. ___ chili peppers

24 Complete the dialogue.

Tina: Hi, Mom. I'm so hungry! Can I have a snack?

Mom: Have some fruit.

Tina: Is there any watermelon?

Mom: I don't think so.

Tina: _____ strawberries?

Mom: No. What about an apple?

Tina: No, thanks. _____ cheese?

Mom: Yes, _____.

Tina: Great. I want a cheese sandwich.

Mom: Sorry, but _____ bread.

Tina: _____ yogurt?

Mom: No, there isn't.

Tina: Well, I guess I'll have an apple.

I Can
- ☐ talk about foods I like.
- ☐ talk about things you have or don't have.
- ☐ identify healthy foods.
- ☐ write about breakfast.

unit 8

Healthy LIVING

B23

1 Listen and read. Then sing.

Get Some Exercise!

"Are you feeling well?" asks Mom.
"You don't look good to me."
"I didn't get much sleep," I say.
"I watched too much TV!"

"Did you have breakfast?"
Mom says, "You know I worry."
"Just a candy bar," I say,
"'Cause I was in a hurry."

Sleep right. Eat right.
Be healthy. Live right!

"Did you ride your bike to school?"
Mom says, "It's good for you."
"Dad drove me in his new car.
Mom, he offered to!"

"Let's ride bikes after school,"
Says Mom. "We'll start today."
"But Mom, I do get exercise.
I do some every day.
I play video games and stretch
My fingers as I play!"

(Chorus)

B24

2 Listen. Number both sets of pictures from 1–4.

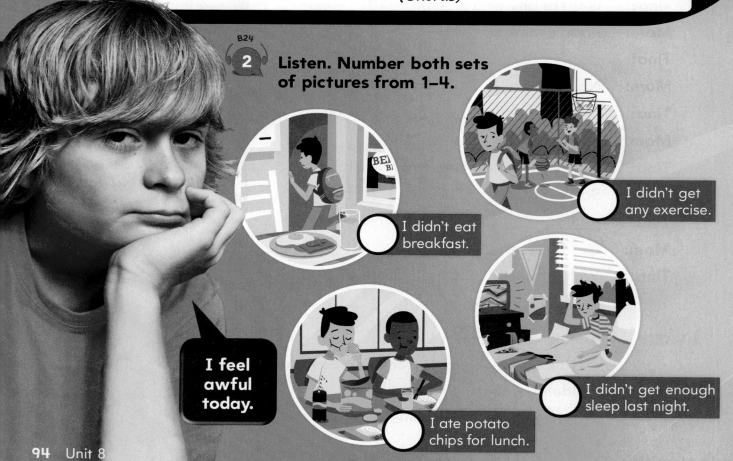

I didn't eat breakfast.

I didn't get any exercise.

I feel awful today.

I didn't get enough sleep last night.

I ate potato chips for lunch.

I feel great today.

I had eggs, toast, and orange juice for breakfast.

I drank lots of water.

I rode my bike after school.

I got ten hours of sleep last night.

THINK BIG

3 Talk about the questions with a partner.

1. Which kid has healthy habits? Explain.
2. Which kid has unhealthy habits? Explain.
3. Are you like the girl or the boy? Explain.

4 B25 Work with a partner. Listen. Ask and answer.

Why does he feel awful today?

Because he didn't get enough sleep.

Did you get enough sleep last night?

Yes, I did.

Story

B26–27
5 **Listen and read.**

A Healthy Dinner

Panel 1

How was your dinner?

Did you eat healthy foods?

Uh...

Kind of...

1 Danny's dad wants Danny to be healthy.

Panel 2

Well, did you eat any vegetables?

Yes, I did. I ate a big burger. It had onions and pickles on it. Onions and pickles are vegetables!

2 Danny likes unhealthy foods.

Panel 3

I guess...

And I ate French fries. Fries are potatoes. They are vegetables, right?

Well, yes, but...

3 Danny likes French fries, but fried foods aren't very healthy.

Panel 4

Did you drink any water?

Well, yes, I did. I had a large soda.

4 Danny likes soda.

5 Danny knows his dinner wasn't really healthy.

6 Now Danny doesn't feel well. He needs to eat healthier foods.

READING COMPREHENSION

6 **Circle _T_ for _true_ or _F_ for _false_.**

	True	False
1. Danny doesn't like many vegetables.	T	F
2. Drinking a lot of soda is healthy.	T	F
3. French fries are good for you.	T	F
4. Potatoes are vegetables.	T	F
5. Danny's dad is happy about Danny's dinner.	T	F

THINK BIG **7** **Talk about the questions with a partner.**

1. What does Danny's father want Danny to do?
2. How does Danny feel after dinner? Why?
3. What healthy foods do you like to eat? Explain.
4. What unhealthy foods do you like to eat? Explain.

B28

8 Listen and read. Say.

Tomas:	Hi, Mariela. How are you?
Mariela:	I feel great today! I got lots of sleep. I ate a good breakfast. How about you?
Tomas:	I don't feel good today.
Mariela:	Why? Did you eat breakfast?
Tomas:	Yes, I did. I ate three donuts.
Mariela:	Three donuts! That's why you feel bad!

9 Practice the dialogue in **8** with a partner. Use the activities on pages 94–95.

B29

10 Listen and stick.

Peggy Saturday Sunday

Carlos Saturday Sunday

| Did you/he/she/they **get** enough sleep yesterday? | Yes, I/he/she/they **did**. | No, I/he/she/they **didn't**. |

11 **Complete the dialogues. Use *did* or *didn't*.**

1. **A:** Good morning, Katia. _____ you eat breakfast?

   B: Yes, I _____.

2. **A:** _____ Ted take a shower this morning?

   B: No, he _____.

3. **A:** _____ the lacrosse team get enough sleep before the game?

   B: No, they _____.

4. **A:** _____ Melissa brush her teeth?

   B: Yes, she _____.

12 **Look at the chart. Write questions and answers about Becca.**

Becca's Habits	Mon	Tue	Wed	Thu	Fri
1. ate a healthy breakfast	✓		✓	✓	
2. got enough exercise		✓			✓
3. got enough sleep	✓	✓	✓		

1. (sleep / Monday) _Did Becca get enough sleep on Monday?_

   Yes, _____

2. (exercise / Friday) _____

   Yes, _____

3. (healthy breakfast / Tuesday) _____

   No, _____

13 **Talk about your habits. Ask and answer with a partner.**

Did you get enough exercise today?

No, I didn't.

CONTENT WORDS

activities	body	calorie
gain weight	measure	pay attention

14 **Listen and read.**

What Is a Calorie?

A calorie is a measure of the energy you get from food. Your body needs a certain number of calories to do all the things you do every day. But if you eat more calories than your body needs, you can gain weight.

How Many Calories Do You Need?

Most people need 1,600 to 2,500 calories every day to stay in shape. Activities such as playing sports, dancing, and bike riding use a lot of calories. Sleeping and watching TV do not use many calories. Pay attention to how many calories you eat and how many calories you use each day.

Activity	Calories used per hour
sleeping	60
watching TV	75
walking	230
dancing	270
swimming	520
running	700
riding a bike	710

15 **Look at the chart and answer the questions.**

1. How many calories do you use when you swim for an hour? _____

2. Running for two hours uses 1,400 calories. True or false? _____

3. How many calories does sleeping for ten hours use? _____

4. Which activity uses more calories—swimming or running? _____

16 **Choose three activities you like to do. Complete the chart with your own information.**

Activity	Number of hours	Total calories used

B37

17 Listen and read.

Strange Sports

Almost everyone knows about soccer, baseball, and basketball. But do you know anything about octopush, footvolley, or pumpkin regattas? Read about these strange sports!

Octopush

Octopush comes from England, but people now play it all over the world. Octopush is like hockey, but people play it under water. Players use a small stick. They try to push a puck into a net to score points for their team.

Footvolley

Footvolley is a sport from Brazil. Footvolley is like volleyball, but the players use a soccer ball. Players have to pass the ball to the other team over a high net. They cannot touch the ball with their hands. People play footvolley on the beach. It is very exciting but very difficult!

Pumpkin Regatta

Each fall, in parts of the United States and Canada, people join in a contest called a pumpkin regatta. It is like a boat race, but the players do not race in boats. They race in giant, hollowed out pumpkins! These pumpkins weigh more than 450 kilograms (1,000 pounds). After the race, there's a pumpkin pie-eating contest.

18 THINK BIG **Talk about the questions with a partner.**

1. Which sports do you like to play? Explain.

2. Are you a member of any sports clubs in your school? Which ones?

3. Which of the three "strange sports" sounds fun to you? Explain.

Use *and*, *but*, and *or* to combine two simple sentences into one compound sentence.

> I went to bed at 9:00. I woke up at 7:00.
> ⟶ I went to bed at 9:00, **and** I woke up at 7:00.

> Dad ate oatmeal. Mom didn't eat breakfast.
> ⟶ Dad ate oatmeal, **but** Mom didn't eat breakfast.

> We can walk to the store. We can take the bus.
> ⟶ We can walk to the store, **or** we can take the bus.

19 **Circle the words *and*, *but*, and *or* in the paragraph.**

I don't like to play sports, but I need to get exercise. I like walking, and I walk to school every day. My dad goes hiking on the weekend, or he goes to the gym. I like to go to the gym with him. He lifts weights, and I walk on the treadmill. For a treat afterward, we go out for smoothies, or we make tacos at home. Dad makes the best tacos, but Mom's cooking is good, too.

20 **Join the simple sentences to make compound sentences. Use the word in parentheses.**

1. My sister plays soccer. My brother plays baseball. *(and)*

   <u>My sister plays soccer, and my brother plays baseball.</u>

2. I usually eat eggs in the morning. Today I had pancakes. *(but)*

   _____

3. We can have chicken for dinner. We can try the new restaurant. *(or)*

   _____

4. Freddie can run two miles. He doesn't run fast. *(but)*

   _____

5. We can ride our bikes. Then we can go out for pizza. *(and)*

   _____

21 **In your notebook, write three compound sentences about healthy habits. Use *and*, *but*, and *or* one time each.**

B32

22 Look and listen. Check (✓) the healthy activities.

☐ 1.   ☐ 2.   ☐ 3.   ☐ 4.

23 Work with a partner. Tell your partner to do healthy things.

> Don't watch TV. Go outside and play soccer!

> Ride your bike at a park or in your neighborhood. It's fun, and it's good for you.

PROJECT

24 Work with a group. Think of a new game you can play outside. Write down the rules. Teach the rest of the class your new game.

B33

25 Listen and complete the questions. Then ask three classmates the questions and write their answers in the chart. Report their answers to the class.

Questions	Student 1: _____	Student 2: _____	Student 3: _____
1. Did you _____ your teeth today?	1.	1.	1.
2. Did you _____ a healthy breakfast?	2.	2.	2.
3. Did you _____ enough sleep last night?	3.	3.	3.
4. Did you _____ enough exercise last week?	4.	4.	4.
5. Did you _____ a shower yesterday?	5.	5.	5.
6. Did you _____ enough water today?	6.	6.	6.

Rob didn't get enough sleep last night.

Bryan didn't drink enough water today.

26 **Circle the correct verb.**

1. Lenny is tired. He didn't **get / got** enough sleep last night.

2. I **eat / ate** a bowl of ice cream for breakfast. I feel sick.

3. She's thirsty. She didn't **drink / drank** enough water today.

4. We **go / went** biking with our friends yesterday. It was fun.

27 **Read the sentence. Make a check for *healthy*. Write an *X* for *unhealthy*.**

☐ 1. I was so busy yesterday. I didn't eat breakfast.

☐ 2. The team drank lots of water after the race.

☐ 3. She ate lots of fruits and vegetables for lunch.

☐ 4. He played video games all day.

☐ 5. They didn't go to baseball practice today.

28 **Answer the questions about yourself. Write complete sentences.**

1. Did you get enough sleep last night?

_____

2. Did you get enough exercise last weekend?

_____

3. Did you eat a healthy breakfast this morning?

_____

4. Did you drink enough water yesterday?

_____

I Can ☐ talk about healthy and unhealthy habits.
☐ talk about activities in the past.

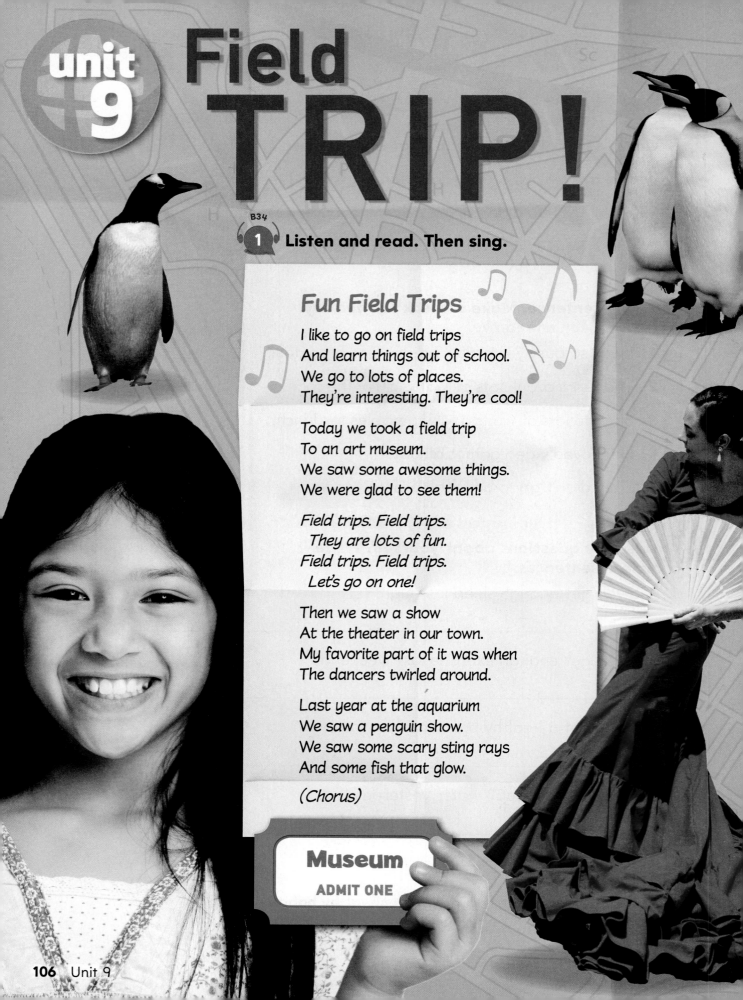

unit 9 Field TRIP!

B34

1 Listen and read. Then sing.

Fun Field Trips

I like to go on field trips
And learn things out of school.
We go to lots of places.
They're interesting. They're cool!

Today we took a field trip
To an art museum.
We saw some awesome things.
We were glad to see them!

Field trips. Field trips.
They are lots of fun.
Field trips. Field trips.
Let's go on one!

Then we saw a show
At the theater in our town.
My favorite part of it was when
The dancers twirled around.

Last year at the aquarium
We saw a penguin show.
We saw some scary sting rays
And some fish that glow.

(Chorus)

Museum
ADMIT ONE

2 Listen. Say the place. Write the activity under each place.

1. science museum

2. art museum

French Paintings

3. theater

4. concert hall

saw a movie _____ _____ _____

5. dairy farm

6. national park

7. zoo

8. aquarium

_____ _____ _____

3 Work with a partner. Listen. Ask and answer.

Where did you go?

What did you do there?

We went to the aquarium.

We saw a penguin show.

Story

B37–38

4 **Listen and read.**

The Awesome Field Trip

1 Megan and Marnie went on a school field trip.

2 Their class went to a big park whe[re] there are very old rocks.

3 Their teacher told them a lot of things about the rocks in the park.

4 Megan liked the park. The field trip was interesting for her.

108 Unit 9

5 Marnie didn't like the field trip. It was boring for her.

6 Marnie hopes she never sees another rock!

READING COMPREHENSION

5 **Read and circle the correct answer.**

1. The twins went to a **museum / national park** for a field trip.

2. On the field trip, the girls learned about **animals / rocks**.

3. Marnie thought the field trip was **interesting / boring**.

4. Megan thought the field trip was **interesting / boring**.

6 **THINK BIG** **Talk about the questions with a partner.**

1. Did Marnie like the field trip? Why or why not?

2. Did Megan like the field trip? Why or why not?

3. Was Marnie happy with Megan's present? Why or why not?

4. What kind of field trips do you like? Explain.

B39

7 Listen and read. Say.

Grandpa:	What did you do at school today?
Susana:	We went on a field trip.
Grandpa:	Oh, that's nice. Where did you go?
Susana:	We went to the aquarium.
Grandpa:	What did you do there?
Susana:	We got to pet baby sharks.
Grandpa:	Did you like the aquarium?
Susana:	Yes, I liked it a lot. It was really cool!

8 Practice the dialogue in **7** with a partner. Use the places on pages 106–107.

B40

9 Listen and stick.

Where **did** you/he/she/they **go**?	I/He/She/They **went** to the Museum of Science.	
What **did** you/he/she/they **see**?	I/He/She/They **saw** an interesting movie about dinosaurs.	
Did you/he/she/they **like** it?	Yes, I/he/she/they **liked** it.	No, I /he/she/they **didn't like** it.

10 **Complete the dialogue.**

A: Where _____ you go yesterday?

B: I _____ to see a movie.

A: What _____ you see?

B: I _____ that new horror movie.

A: _____ you like it?

B: No, I _____ it. It was too scary.

11 **Read and match. Make sentences.**

_____ **1.** We went to a dairy farm   **a.** the play.

_____ **2.** What did you see   **b.** go yesterday?

_____ **3.** She didn't like   **c.** like rock music.

_____ **4.** Where did you   **d.** to learn about milking cows.

_____ **5.** I don't really   **e.** at the natural history museum?

12 **THINK BIG** **Work with a partner. Ask and answer questions. Use the words from the box.**

last weekend   last year   yesterday

Where did you go yesterday?

I went to the art museum.

CONTENT WORDS
beautiful   boring   funny   interesting   scary   strange

B41

13 Look at the paintings. Listen.

At the Museum

1. *Breezing Up* by Winslow Homer

2. *The Scream* by Edvard Munch

3. *Big Circus* by Marc Chagall

4. *Self-Portrait with Thorn Necklace and Hummingbird* by Frida Kahlo

THINK BIG

14 Work with a partner. Talk about the paintings in **13**. Use the words from the box.

I saw a painting by Edvard Munch. It's called *The Scream*.

Did you like it?

No, I didn't. It was scary!

15 Listen and read.

The World Stage

Today, people everywhere enjoy watching movies and television. But before movies and television, people went to the theater to see dance or plays. Here are a few different kinds of theater from around the world.

Flamenco

Flamenco is a kind of dance from Spain. It started hundreds of years ago, but people still enjoy watching and performing flamenco today. Flamenco music and dance are very dramatic. Together, the music and dance tell a story.

Mau Roi Nuoc

In Vietnam, there's an interesting kind of theater called *Mau Roi Nuoc*. There are no actors—only puppets. The puppets are on a stage filled with water. Mau Roi Nuoc started hundreds of years ago, but people still enjoy watching the shows today.

Shakespeare's Plays

William Shakespeare wrote many plays in England about 400 years ago. You can see his plays all over the world today. One of his most famous plays is *Romeo and Juliet*. In the 1600s, Shakespeare's plays were very popular. In those days, all of the parts were played by men.

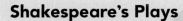

16 THINK **BIG** **Work with a partner. Ask and answer.**

1. Have you ever been to the theater? What did you see?

2. What kinds of performances do you like?

3. Which of the kinds of theater shown here would you like to see? Why?

Read the sentences. See how the verbs agree with the subjects.

The girl **dances**.	The children **dance**.
She **does** not **sing**.	They **do** not **sing**.
The girl **danced**.	The children **danced**.
She **did** not **sing**.	They **did** not **sing**.

Read the sentences. See how the *be* verbs agree with the subjects.

I **am** a student.	He **is** my brother. He **is** my sister.	We You They	**are** cold.
I **am** not a teacher.	He **is** not my cousin. She **is** not my cousin.	We You They	**are** not hot.

I He She	**was** happy.	We You They	**were** at school.
I He She	**was** not sad.	We You They	**were** not at home.

17 **Circle the correct verb.**

1. I **doesn't / don't** like peas.

2. Meg **go / goes** to art class.

3. They **is / are** my friends.

4. He **is / are** a good student.

5. We **doesn't / don't** play soccer.

6. You **isn't / aren't** hungry.

18 **Complete the sentences. Use the *past* form of the verb in parentheses.**

1. Paul _____ *went* _____ to school today. (go)

2. I _____ here at 3:00. (be)

3. We _____ breakfast this morning. (eat)

4. They _____ the movie. (not see)

5. Sandra _____ in science class today. (not be)

19 **Write the words from the box in the chart.**

> basketball   dance   drawing   English   math   painting   science   soccer   swimming

Sports	Arts	School Subjects

20 **Work with a partner. Talk about your talents.**

 Do you like math?

No, I don't. But I like art! I'm good at painting.

PROJECT

21 **Have a talent show. Share your talent with the class.**

Class Talent Show

B43

22 Listen and complete the chart.

	1. Lucia	2. Gerald	3. Gwen	4. Mickey
went to	aquarium			
saw	fish and other animals			
liked/didn't like it	liked it			

23 Make up your own field trip. Answer the questions.

1. Where did you go? _____

2. What did you see? _____

3. Did you like it? Why or why not? _____

24 Ask your classmates about their field trips. Take notes in your notebook. Say who had the most interesting field trip.

Sandra went to a toy museum. She saw some very old toys. Some of them were a hundred years old! She liked it a lot.

25 **Write the places. Use the words from the box.**

| aquarium | art museum | concert hall | dairy farm |
| national park | science museum | theater | zoo |

1. _____ 2. _____ 3. _____ 4. _____

5. _____ 6. _____ 7. _____ 8. _____

26 **Complete the dialogue.**

A: Hey! How are you, Susie?

B: I'm fine, Dad.

A: What did you _____ today?

B: I _____ on a field trip with my class.

A: Cool! Where did you _____?

B: We went to the zoo.

A: That sounds fun. Did you _____ it?

B: Yes. I _____. It _____ really fun!

I Can ☐ talk about actions in the past.

☐ ask for and give opinions about activities.

Checkpoint | Units 7–9

How Well Do I Know It? Can I Use It?

1 Think about it. Read and circle. Practice.

😊 I know this.   😐 I need more practice.   😟 I don't know this.

	PAGES			
Food: bread, ham, lettuce, onions, sandwich . . .	82–83	😊	😐	😟
Healthy habits: ate breakfast, drank water, got enough sleep, rode my bike . . .	94–95	😊	😐	😟
Field-trip places: aquarium, science museum, national park, theater . . .	107	😊	😐	😟
Field-trip activities: saw a penguin show, saw a movie, learned about rocks, saw a play . . .	107	😊	😐	😟
Is there **any** pizza? No, there isn't **any** pizza. There are **some** sandwiches.	86–87	😊	😐	😟
Did you **get** enough exercise? Yes, I **did**. **Did** you **get** enough sleep? No, I **didn't**.	98–99	😊	😐	😟
Where **did** they **go**? They **went** to the zoo. What **did** they **see**? They **saw** a parrot show. **Did** they **like** it? Yes, they **liked** it.	110–111	😊	😐	😟

B44

2 **Get ready.**

A. Complete the dialogue. Write the numbers of Kelly's answers on the correct lines. Then listen and check.

Kelly: Hello?

Dad: Hi, Kelly. It's Dad.

Kelly: Oh, hi, Dad!

Dad: How is New York City?

Kelly: _____

Dad: What did you do yesterday?

Kelly: _____

Dad: That sounds fun. Did you like it?

Kelly: _____

Dad: Great. So, when is your soccer game?

Kelly: _____

Dad: I see. Did you get enough sleep last night?

Kelly: _____

Dad: That's good. Did you eat breakfast this morning?

Kelly: _____

Dad: That sounds delicious! Well, good luck today. Call me after your game.

Kelly: OK, Dad. Talk to you later.

Dad: Bye.

Kelly's answers

1. Yes, Dad. I ate a breakfast burrito. It was stuffed with eggs, cheese, rice, and beans.

2. Yes, it was great! We saw a lot of interesting paintings.

3. Yes, I went to bed at 7:00 last night.

4. We went to the Museum of Modern Art.

5. It's today. It starts at 2:00.

6. It's really cool. We arrived yesterday afternoon.

B. Practice the dialogue in **A** with a partner. Then practice again. Make up your own answers.

1
2
3
4
5
6
7
8
9

3 **Get set.**

STEP 1 Cut out the cards on page 127.

STEP 2 Read Dialogue 1 below. Then place the cards in order to create Dialogue 2.

STEP 3 Look at the pictures below. Choose the picture that illustrates each dialogue. Now you're ready to **Go!**

4 **Go!**

A. With a partner, practice Dialogue 1. Change parts and practice again.

A: Where did you go yesterday?

B: We went to a big art museum.

A: What did you do there?

B: We looked at some paintings.

A: Did you like it?

B: Not really. The paintings were strange.

A: What did you eat for dinner?

B: I ate four slices of pizza.

A: Did you get enough sleep last night?

B: No. I went to bed at around 11:00.

A: Did you eat breakfast this morning?

B: No. I drank some water. I feel kind of sick.

> Where did you go yesterday?

> We went to a big art museum.

B. Use your cards to act out Dialogue 2 with a partner.

5 **Write about yourself.**

- Where did you go last weekend?
- What did you do there?
- Did you like it?

- Did you get enough sleep last night?
- Did you eat a healthy breakfast?

All About Me   Date:_____

_____

_____

_____

_____

_____

_____

_____

_____

How Well Do I Know It Now?

6 **Think about it.**

A. Go to page 118. Read and circle again. Use a different color.

B. Check (✔).

☐ I can ask my teacher for help.

☐ I can practice.

7 **Rate this Checkpoint. Color the stars.**

 very easy   easy   hard   very hard   fun   not fun

ask a question with:

What time . . .

ask a question with:

When . . .

ask a question with:

**in the morning /
afternoon / evening**

ask a question with:

**at _____:_____
(time)**

ask a question with:

before work

ask a question with:

after work

answer with:

I . . .

answer with:

I always . . .

answer with:

I usually . . .

answer with:

I sometimes . . .

answer with:

I never . . .

answer with:

I have to . . .

All About _____
(animals)

_____ can
(animals)

_____
(activity)

But they can't _____
(activity)

4

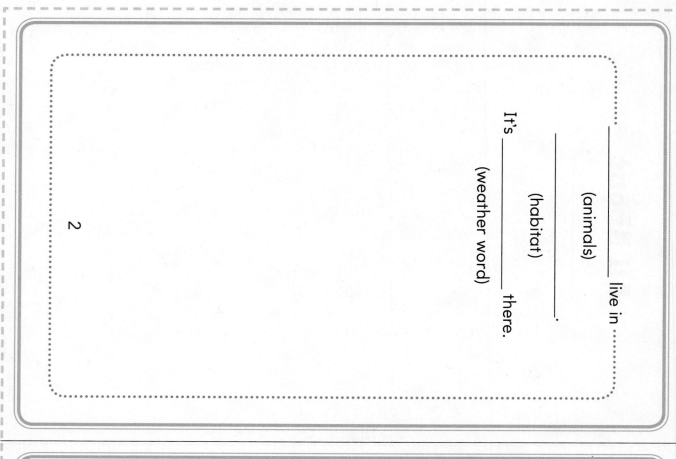

_____ live in
(animals)
_____ .
(habitat)
It's _____ there.
(weather word)

2

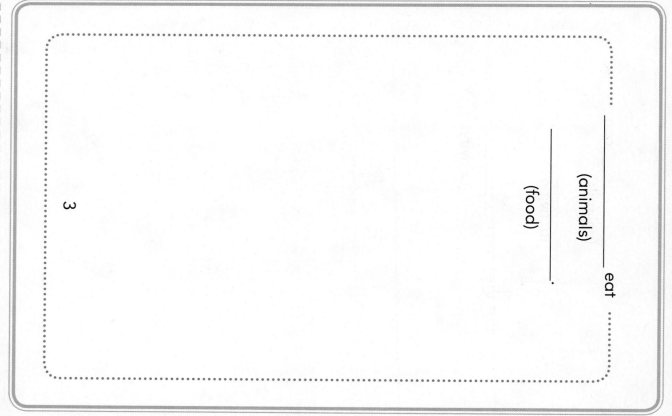

_____ eat
(animals)
_____ .
(food)

3

Dialogue 2

A: Did you eat breakfast this morning?

B: Yes, it was awesome. Sharks are cool!

A: Did you like it?

B: I ate chicken, rice, and salad.

A: What did you do there?

B: Yes, I had yogurt, fruit, and toast. I'm ready for the baseball game!!

A: What did you eat for dinner?

B: We went to the aquarium.

A: Where did you go yesterday?

B: We saw a movie about sharks.

Young Learners English
Movers

Practice Materials
Sampler

Note to students:

These practice materials will help you prepare for the YLE (Young Learners English) Tests.

There are three kinds of tests in this sampler: Listening, Reading & Writing, and Speaking.

Good luck!

Listening A

B45

– 5 questions –

Listen and check (✔) the box. There is one example.

What is his job?

A ☐

B ☑

C ☐

1   What is her job?

A ☐

B ☐

C ☐

2   What time does she usually stop working?

A ☐

B ☐

C ☐

3 What does she have to do every day?

A ☐

B ☐

C ☐

4 What does she like about her job?

A ☐

B ☐

C ☐

5 What job would she like to have in the future?

A ☐

B ☐

C ☐

Listening B

– 5 questions –

Listen and draw lines. There is one example.

Mary   John   Vicky   Fred

Jack   Sally

– 5 questions –

Listen and write. There is one example.

Susie's Field Trip

What Susie did today: _____went on a field trip_____

1 Where she went: _____

2 What she did in the morning: _____

3 What she had for lunch: _____

4 What she did in the afternoon: _____

5 What she learned: _____

Reading & Writing A

Read the story. Choose a word from the box. Write the correct word next to numbers 1–6. There is one example.

Today starts off like any other day for Paul. He _____ *wakes up* _____
and gets out of bed. Then he goes into the bathroom and
(1) _____. After that he (2) _____
and takes the bus to school. But something is different today. At
lunch he doesn't have to wait in line. The other kids let him go to
the front. After school Paul comes home. He usually has to
(3) _____ and take him for a walk, but today his
sister does it for him. In the evening, Paul's mom cooks his favorite
dinner. He always has to (4) _____ after dinner,
but today he gets a break. Instead of doing chores, he gets to
(5) _____ with his brother and sister. What's
different about today? It's Paul's birthday. He almost always
(6) _____ at 8 o'clock, but today his parents let
him stay up late and eat ice cream. "I wish every day was like
today," says Paul.

example

wakes up	eats breakfast	play soccer
wash dishes	does homework	goes to bed
washes his face	feed the dog	play games

(7) Now choose the best name for the story.

Check (✔) one box.

My Everyday Life ☐

A Very Special Day ☐

Time for a Break ☐

Reading & Writing B

Read the text. Choose the right words and write them on the lines.

Example   Bears live in many different kinds of places
around the _____world_____. Some bears
live in forests and mountains. Grizzly bears,
for example, live in the Rocky Mountains,
in the United States. They explore when the

1 _____ is warm, and they sleep during
2 the long winter. They _____ climb
trees and catch fish.

Polar bears live in the Arctic, where it's
3 _____ and cold all year round. They
4 have thick _____ to protect them
from the cold, and they hunt for fish under
5 the _____. Like all other bears, they
fit right into their environment.

Example ocean desert world

1 weather   water   world
2 can   should   will

3 snowy   hot   rainy
4 feathers   beaks   fur

5 rock   ice   wood

Reading & Writing C

– 6 questions –

Look and read. Write yes or no.

Examples

It's cold and windy today.   no

People are watching a play.   yes

Questions

1 A woman is jogging. _____

2 A family is having a picnic. _____

3 There are some sandwiches on a plate. _____

4 A girl is walking her dog. _____

5 People are watching a movie. _____

6 There is some lemonade for sale. _____

Speaking A

  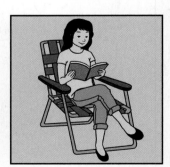

Unit 1, page 6

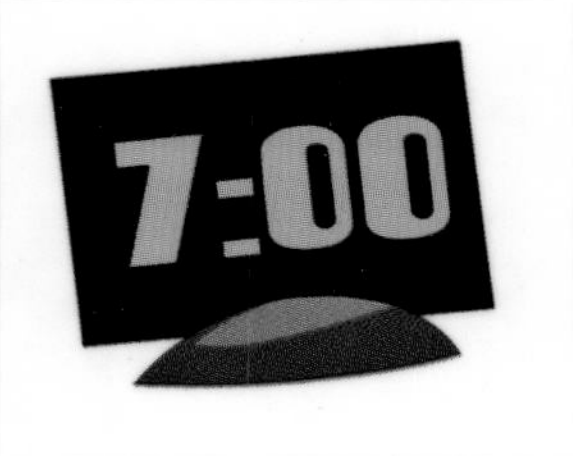

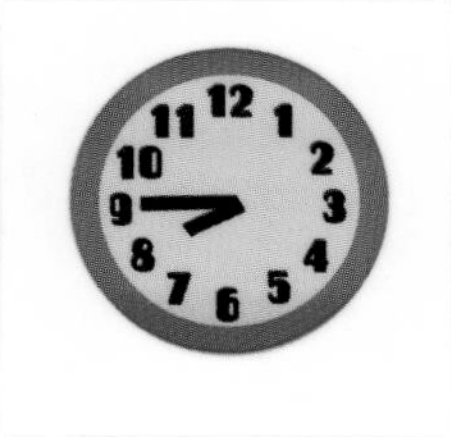
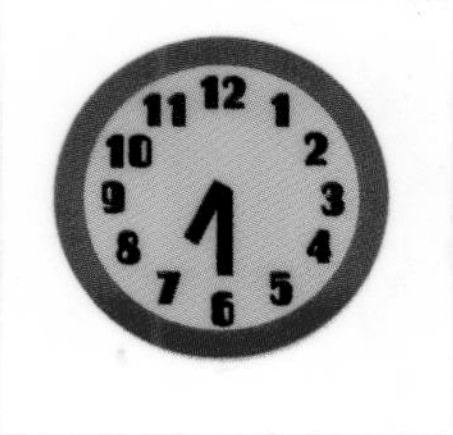
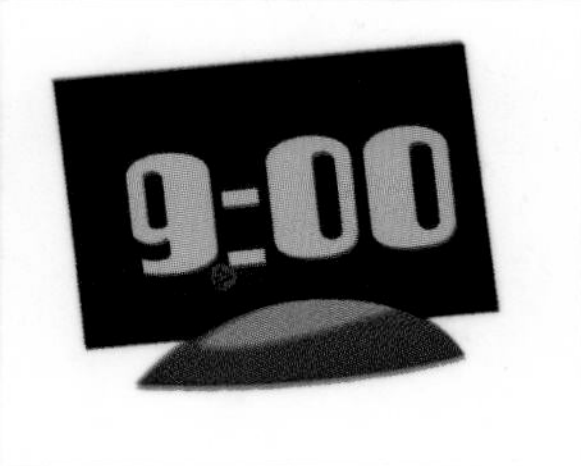

Unit 2, page 18

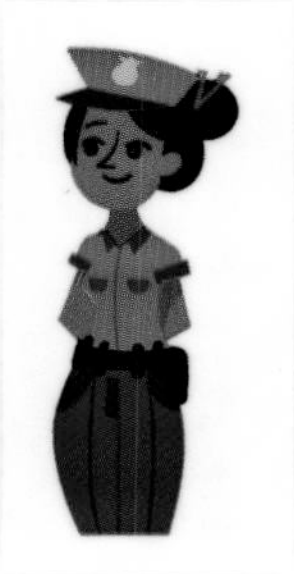
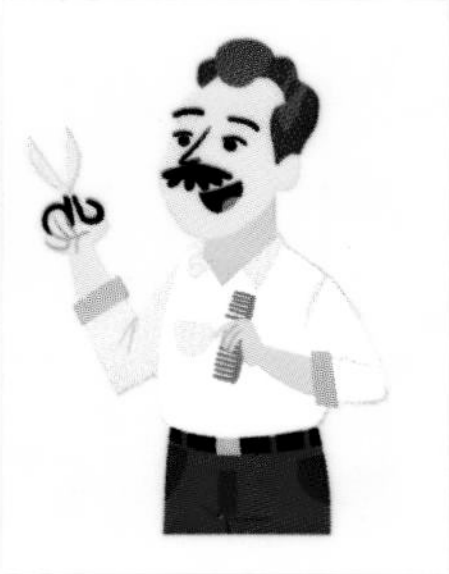
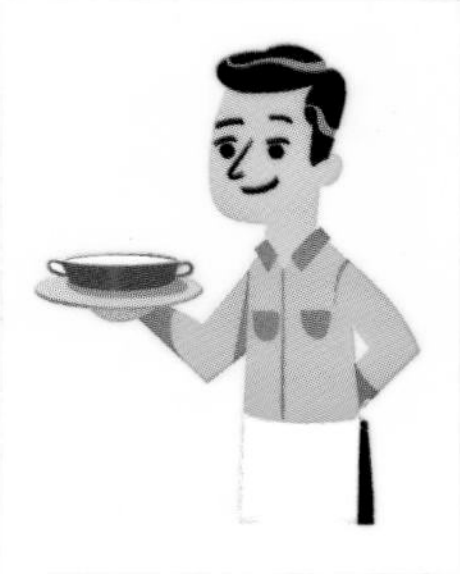
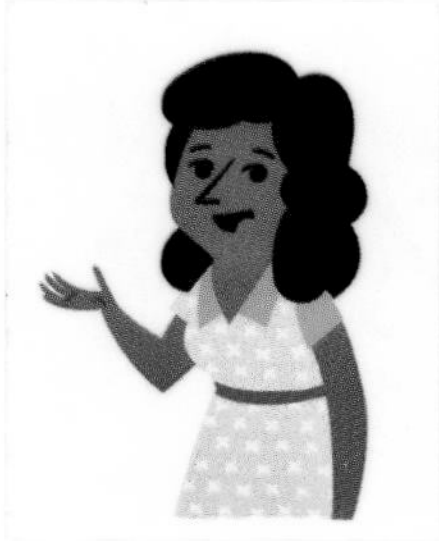

Unit 3, page 30

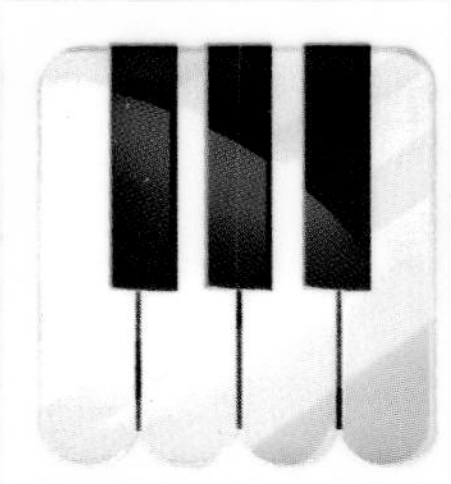

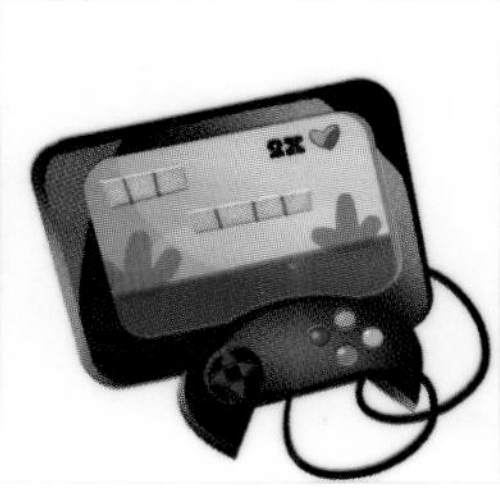
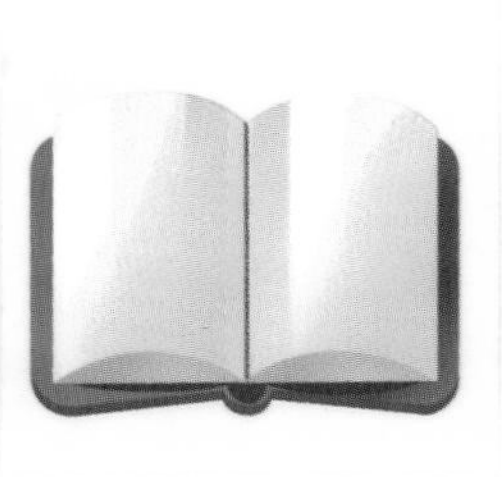
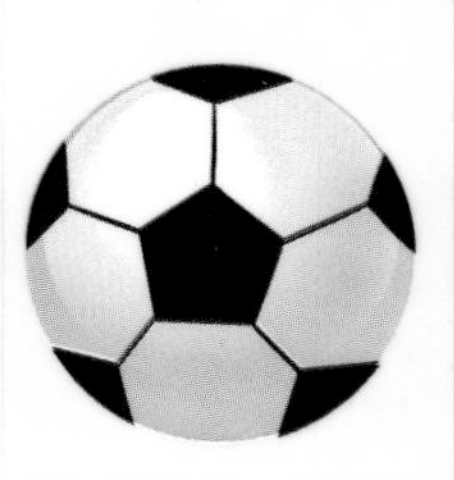

Unit 4, page 46

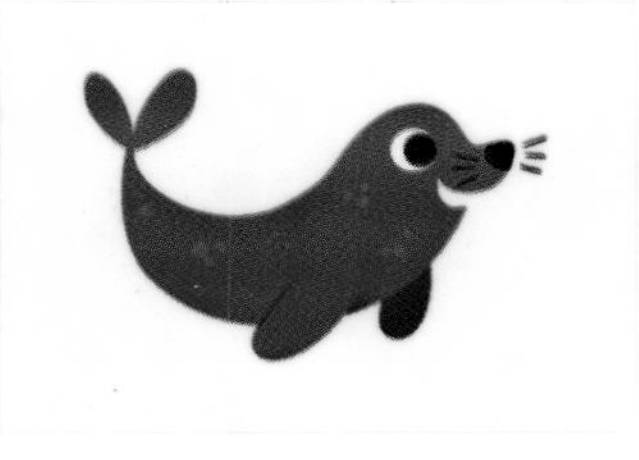
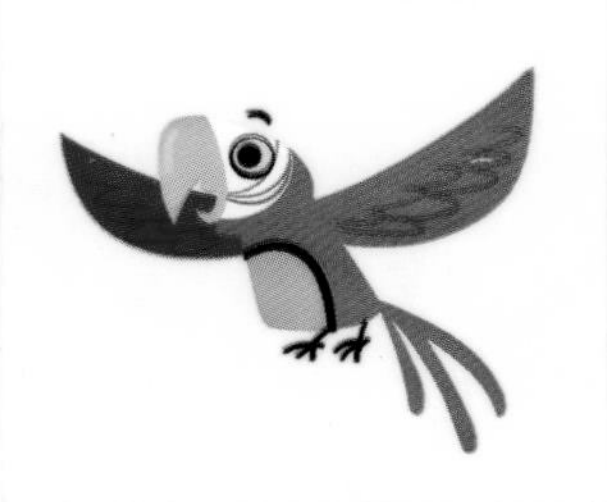
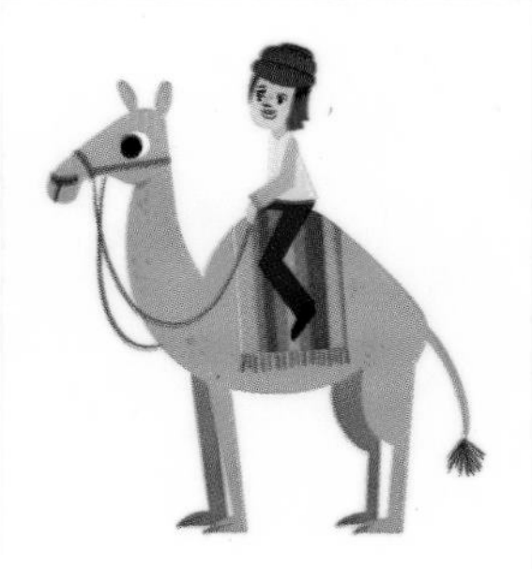
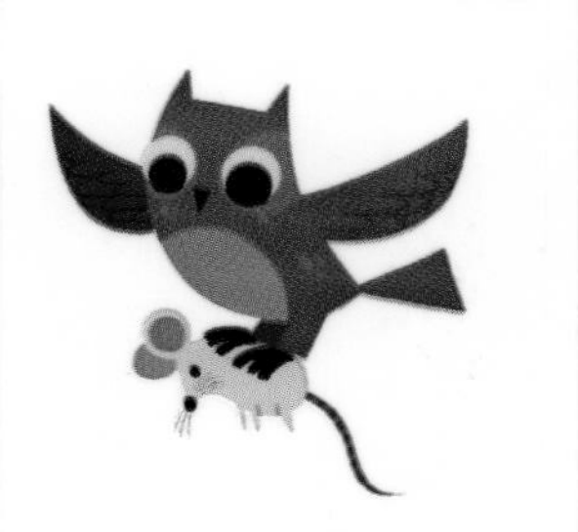

Unit 5, page 58

Unit 6, page 70

Unit 7, page 86

Unit 8, page 98

Unit 9, page 110